MORE COLLECTED POEMS

Hugh MacDiarmid

More Collected Poems

MACGIBBON & KEE

FIRST PUBLISHED 1970 BY MACGIBBON & KEE LTD
3 UPPER JAMES STREET GOLDEN SQUARE LONDON W1
COPYRIGHT © CHRISTOPHER MURRAY GRIEVE 1970
PRINTED IN GREAT BRITAIN BY
EBENEZER BAYLIS & SON LTD
THE TRINITY PRESS
WORCESTER AND LONDON

SBN 261 63172 1

CONTENTS

AUTHOR'S NOTE

When my *Collected Poems* was published in the USA and Scotland in 1962, the title was wrong, since publishing expediences had led to only a portion of the poems submitted being used. The book was therefore only a big selection of my poems. Some of the poems excluded in this way I have since had published in *A Lap of Honour* and *A Clyack-Sheaf*, but the bulk of them has remained uncollected till now. The poems in this volume were not included in *Collected Poems* and are collected here for the first time.

Biggar March 1970   HUGH MACDIARMID

There is No Movement in the World like Yours

There is nae movement in the warld like yours.
You are as different frae a'thing else
As water frae a book, fear frae the stars . . .
The licht that History sheds on onything
Is naething to the licht you shed on it.
Time's dourest riddles to solution slide
Like Lautréamont's cormorant: and Man
Shudders to see you slippin' into place . . .
The simple explanations that you gi'e
O' age-lang mysteries are little liked
Even by them wha best appreciate
The soond advice you gied to Mither Eve,
        Or think they dae.

The beneficiaries o' incredible change
Are naturally conservative, even as
Resetters o' ancestral loot are aye
Strang on the Law. The horror maist folk feel
On seein' you is natural eneuch.
There is nae movement in the warld like yours
Save faith's, that can move mountains, gin it shak's
The grund 'neath its ain feet for practice whiles
And there's nae sayin' what'll happen neist.
Man sees the changin' warld and feel changed tae
Like ane wha sittin' in a standin' train
Sees anither pass, and thinks it's his that's gaen
        And fegs it is!

Poets in throes o' composition whiles
See you as fishermen in favourite pools
May see a muckle fish they canna catch

gin, if   neist, next
        fegs! faith!

Clood-like beneath the glitterin' fry they can,
Contra nando incrementum lyin'
Under the roarin' cataracts o' Life,
Like the catalysis that underlies
A' the illusions o' romantic love.
Poets! – to whom a yellow primrose is
A yellow primrose, and nae mair, or less!
– Can you be in their harns and no' the pool
Yet wi' a sudden bowspring on the air
    Ootshine the sun?

The dooble tongue has spoken and been heard.
What poet has repeated ocht it said?
There is nae movement in the warld like yours.
Vain is the image o' Leviathan
And vain the image o' reflectit throes,
For you rin coonter to the rhythms o' thocht,
Wreched oot o' recognition a' words fail
To haud you, alien to the human mind,
Yet in your ain guid time you suddenly slip,
Nae man kens hoo, into the simplest phrase,
While a' the diction'ry rejoices like
The hen that saw its ugly ducklin' come
    Safe to the shore again.

Come let us face the facts. We ken that there's
Nae invocation that's no' fause but this.
Christ saw you when he said that 'Wha believe
In me shall dae like me – *and greater things.*'
He is nae Christian that's fa'n short o' this,
But och Christ tint you in the seein' tae.
Come let us face the facts. He should ha' socht

harns, brains	ocht, anything
coonter, counter	haud, hold
kens, knows	hoo, how
fause, false	tint, lost

Faith in themsel's like his – no' faith in him.
His words condemned his followers, and himsel',
(Dostoevski ev'n, preferrin' Christ to truth)
And we ha'e seen through twenty centuries syne
Nocht but the lang withdrawal o' the licht
That kythed in him, as 'twere an ebbin' sea
That leaves ahint a waste o' mudflats till
    It come again.

A sorry metaphor, for ony sea
Covers or uncovers the same bed o' glaur
Even as the ebb and flow o' life and art
Leaves the dreich mob unchanged – gin you're no' there.
There is nae movement in the warld like yours
Save sic divergences as dinna leave
Things a' the mair the same the mair they change
But alter them forever in a way
Unheralded and unbelievable
As gin the tide-toucht mud becam' a tune,
A sky, a problem in psychology,
Or something unimaginable as them
    Gin they'd no' been

A'thing on earth repeats itsel' but you
And a'thing langs to pit an end to change.
The praise o' you is no' for any man
Wha seeks to big Jerusalem onywhaur
And be at ease, for he's nae suner there
Than roond its wa's your fatal music dirls
And doon they coup like Jericho's again.

syne, since	nocht, nothing
kythed, appeared	ahint, behind
glaur, mud	dreich, drab
sic, such	langs, longs
big, build	onywhaur, anywhere
coup, fall	

Vain sorrow hides your enigmatic gleam
Cleavin' through ilka confidence owrethrawn,
Through ilka difference and decay and daith
Streight as an arrow on its endless way
Or like a fire that spreids in secret till
          Its haud's complete.

And mairtyrs to their ain stupidity
You set Earth's generations a' alowe
And the neist victim lauchs or grues to see
His predecessor in the acid licht.
The residue o' gowd is unco sma'
And centuries gang to mak' a single grain
While a' the dross o' pomp and circumstance
Burns clear awa' as it had never been.
The hopes and fears o' a' but twa-three men
At best are foolish first, syne null and void.
– O Holy Office, be mair vigorous still
And shrivel up the sameness still to be
          Afore it's born!

As Shelley in the Hoose o' Commons shrieked
In horror at the bestial shapes seen there
Perpetuatin' needless poverty
And mindlessness and fraud and curst conceit
Sae a' the warld is manifest in you
– Religion, Art, Commerce and Industry,
Social and Sexual Relationships,
A' to be lauched at wi' contempt or lang,
Like Queen Victoria or Locarno noo
Or mercifully forgotten – yet your flame
Riddles but canna ridicule Shelley

ilka, each	alowe, ablaze
grues, shakes with disgust	gowd, gold
unco, very	or, before

And Buddha's still a solid darkness in't
      And Christ a live controversy.

Buddha, no' India! Christ and no' the Kirk!
Yet they maun baith be sune forgotten tae
And a' the Past be juist a wisp o' strae
Thrawn on the bonfire that the thocht o' ye lichts.
There is nae mystery in Life or Daith
Save as man mak's it by his ignorance
(Which sers its purpose to your hidden growth),
Your coils are no' at variance tho' they seem
And a'thing fa's into place at last
Wit turns to ignorance, laughter to the joke.
You mak' a concertina o' the sun
      And cut a' airts at aince.

A' airts at aince – but life is faur owre slow,
And freedom inconceivable to man.
Licht moves a thousand times faster than his nerves,
His een are neist to blin', his ears to deef.
It tak's a Dostoevski to believe
And disbelieve a thing at aince, and that's
A puir beginning to *your* cantrips, fegs,
Tho' snails may dream that they'll be eagles yet,
Men Gods and that the unkent future's set
Plain as a pikestaff tho' they canna see't
(And no' – Heaven help us – undecided yet!)
As life is to a bairn afore it kens
      Whether it's Broon's or Smith's . . .

I blink at Yeats as micht a man whom some
Foul sorcery had changed into a pig,
At Yeats, my kingly cousin, and mind hoo

maun, must	baith, both
sers, serves	airts, directions
aince, once	

He prophesied that Eire 'ud hae nae Burns
(Tho' it has tried to mair than aince) but haud
Its genius heich and lanely – and think o' Burns,
That Langfellow in a' but leid, and hoo
Scots since has tint his maikless vir but hains
His cheap emotions, puir ideas, and
Imperfect sense o' beauty, till my race
Lack ev'n the foetus' luck o' Smith or Broon
(A Hobson's choice to burst nae pigskin owre)
        Bein' a' Jock Tamson's bairns.

But weary o' recrimination sune
And in slant licht some movement o' you thraws
See a' the warld become an amber haze,
A sunny flood in which humanity lies
Troot-like, wi' motionin' fins and beckonin' tail,
And wan inscrutable ensnarin' een,
As I've seen often in the Esk or Ewes;
Yet as I look its gantin' mou' becomes,
Clearer than Whistle Binkie bards could draw,
Tho' this was a' the ettle o' their clan,
The waefu' gape o' a wee bairn's smile,
Semihiante labello o' Catullus, there.
        – O my wee troot!

Freedom is *inconceivable*. The word
Betrays the cause – a habit o' the mind,
Thinkin' continually in a certain way,
Generation after generation, till it seems
This is Thocht's fixed unalterable mode;
And here's the reason at aince why human Thocht

heich, high	leid, language
maikless, matchless	vir, energy
hains, keeps	owre, over
Esk, Ewes, rivers in Dumfriesshire	Whistle Binkie, a school of poetasters
ettle, endeavour	waefu', woeful

Is few men's business and sae scant and shawl,
And men hate poems dry and hard and needs
Maun hae them fozy wi' infinity.
'The way a woman walkin' in the street
Kicks oot her skirt ahint her is the thing,
Mair than her soul, gin the exact word's found,
        To gar the Heavens open.'

Then fix the babby in a guid Scots word,
That language no' o' Pan but Peter Pan,
(Christ leuch wi' toom gams aince, the Lord Buddha
Was in a crawl o' bairns aboot the doors)
The dowf and daft-like babby and the way
Its murgeons munk oor manhood and gaup up
Sillier than ever on the face o' Daith.
Mankind ends as it started, mappiemou'd
And never bites aff mair than it can – sook,
And fain, gin Blake was wrang and fools got there,
'Ud mak' an antirrhinum in Heaven at last
        For ither bairns than oors or us.

The poet's hame is in the serpent's mooth,
No' in his ain, or ither man's, or flooer's.
Nae wumman ever had a tongue like this,
No' even the twinklin' aphrodisiac tip
O' Helen's slidin' through her roondit lips
Or Saint Sophia's whisperin' in God's lug
Or subtler members in the warld the day
I aiblins ken owre muckle o', or wull,
Or wad! – subtler, tho' as inferior still

shawl, shallow	fozy, rotten
gar, make	leuch, laughed
toom, empty	gams, gums
dowf, stupid	murgeons, mouth movements
munk, imitate	gaup, gape
mappiemou'd, rabbit-mouthed	sook, suck
lug, ear	aiblins, perhaps

To this as birds' sangs (sae-ca'd) are to men's
Or fancy stuff that's tint its caoin is
To Gaelic music that like Whisky's best
   Ta'en *mar a tha e*

There's ane amang the birds that's perfect, ane
Amang the fish, men say – I kenna which;
My verse bein' fallible's no' poetry yet
And that is a' that I'm concerned aboot.
The consciousness that maitter has entrapped
In minerals, plants and beasts is strugglin' yet
In men's minds only, seekin' to win free,
As poets' ideas, in the fecht wi' words
Forced back upon themsel's and made mair clear,
Owrecome a' thwarts whiles, miracles at last.
Shairly the process should be clear to Scots.
What ither country has a vantage point
   Like Faire na h'Abh?

Few are the Scots that ever heard o't tho'!
Wha stands there sees the gleams (like Cythna's signs,
Clear elemental shapes wha's sma'est change
A subtler language wi'in language mak's
That learners wi' owre muckle *blas na beurl*,
A' tangled up in their *o-hill-i-has*,
Can never seize on!) o' a caulder stream
Than in Avranches' park at peep o' day
Barefut Valéry writin' *Pythia*, found,
Kennin' how nigh impossible it is
To dae ocht worth the daen' and hoo ill
To keep frae wastin' time on ither things,
   And gaed hame drunk wi' will.

It has a look as o' the pooer that's made
The haill warld, whiles, and instantly that's dune

caoin, edge   *mar a tha e*, neat
     haill, whole

18

Turn't to anither and faur harder task,
As micht a poet frae the wark that keeps
His hoosehold bein and lets him turn secure
(Gin only yon *was* easier and left scouth)
       To his true job.

Ignore the silly figure, you that play
Like Arthur Schnabel, to nae gallery,
In programmes, free frae 'fireworks' (as he said
To ane complainin' 'nocht but Schubert!' aince,
'To gi'e folk nae chance to prefer the waur')
Unlike a' ither virtuosos', bein',
(Like you – in anither sense tae, relentless judge)
       'Borin' a' through.'

Here is the task to which it conjures us –
   When man to man the haill warld owre
   Sall brithers be for a' that?
     (I've a sneaky feelin' roond my hert
     That I'm gaen' to settle doon . . .)
   Napoleon near-haund had the poo'er
   To solve the problem Man's workin' at.

   I needs maun think, gin the chance I stake
   O' Gaeldom regained, hoo a' mankind
   Writhes like the cut-up pairts o' a snake
   To jine aince mair - as he'd fain ha'e jined.

   Comparin' wi' his the silly hopes –
   Ex nihil, nihil – sae mony Scots
   Cherish the day, Napoleon's phrase drops
   'Che coglione!' balm on my thoughts!
   'What is Cencrastus but the wriggle

bein, comfortable   waur, worse
jine, join   Cencrastus, great green spot-bellied snake

O' Man's divided vertebrae?
– Gin that were a' I wadna jiggle
For my pairt wi't anither day

For human unity needna mean
Ocht to the problems I'm concerned wi',
Nae anaconda but a green
Kailworm is a' that seems to me.

Messieurs les Anglais, wha preferred
Lenin to Napoleon, see
As sma' again wi that compared
Crawls ev'n your perfidy!

To think nae thocht that's e'er been thocht afore
And nane, that's no' worth mair than a' that ha'e;
And no' be like the Christian folk wha cry
'Religious Truth's been found – a' men can dae's
To feebly reproduce some fragments o't.'
Germans in music – in religion Jews.
Nationality in Algebra even,
Guid kens what savages in nearer things
Cramp and exhaust us in their several spheres,
If we tak' mair than we in turn can gie,
And fail, beneath their natures and oor ain,
And the haill Warld's, to keep the glintin' streams
        O' Unnatural thocht at work.

Ev'n as in writing this, I fear
That aiblins I'm nae mair than thrang
Echoin' some puir German sang
(That was the fashion o' yester-year,
Heringer, Heym, or Zech or Benn,
The sturz and schrei that younger men

thrang, busy

20

In their gehackten Satzen shed
– But can a Scot be well-eneuch read,
*   Alive to Kasach, Loerke, Mell,*
Billinger and mair than I need tell
Or by his nose yet to be led
To end, or no' bide ony langer,
Endlich offen und Empfanger,
Or better still anticipate
The neist sae-ever transient state
And scrawl a phrase frae Scotland yet
On the palimpsest o' th' Infinite?)
Or doot that my cauld current flows
Only frae Husserl, say, and shows
That motion needs maun be explained
Eidetically, or hoo Thocht strained
Through mair and mair ἐχοχάτ gies
The priori o' a' ideas,
While ithers think yon crystal wa'
Merks Heaven . . . or America!

There is nae movement in the warld like yours,
Save his, wha, ere he writes, ken's he'll no' fail
To recognize his dear ev'n tho' her hair
(A'e threid o' which, pu'd through his nails, 'ud frizz
In coontless kinks like Scotland's craziest burn
– Aye, yon bright water even wi' the sky
That if, when we were bairns, we threw corks on't
We panted to keep up wi' thcm in vain)
Whiles loosened owre him like the sun at noon
That insubstantializes a' the warld
Is syne bound, coil on coil in sma'er space
        To show the smoothness o' her brow;
    I saw her in the lilty-beds
    I saw her in the snaw,

pu'd, pulled   frizz, crinkle
                    even, level

21

I saw her in the white sun
That burned the warld awa'

Nor sings o' Barra wha has never seen,
Paedria and Acrasia . . . slipshod wark.

Against Poor Poems with Incomplete Ideas

Then dern nae mair 'neath yon twa-neukit mune
Nor whaur the sunlicht fills the lift wi' gool
– Puir poems concerned wi' incomplete ideas!
Barra, Acrasia – Dr Moreau's Islands!
I see the beast surge up in ilka face.
There is nae man or wumman, reasonable soul,
Frae instinct free and slaves to nae brute law.
A' forms grotesque or comely, gross lines and fine
Athikte wi' a glance reduces still
To the auld balance and bauch interplay.
Orgasms o' common crises – hate, lust, love,
Marriage, parenthood, etcetera.
Men praisin' Nature, and rejoicin' that
They keep their youthfu' spirit to the last,
                    Bourbons and baboons!

I canna be in the Antipodes quick eneuch
At ony minute to keep pace wi' you,
And gin I see it is aye like some
Lateen that comes alang at dusk as though
Impelled by naething but th' advancin' nicht
What is there that lifts up a man's hert mair
Than seein' sic a ship come bowlin' alang
Breist-high towards him, careerin' owre the sea?
It seems to ha' borrowed something o' the air
Something o' the water, and unites them baith,
Their offspring and their bond; but syne I hear
Its sailors like a sparrow's scaldachan
And ken it's in Australia at maist
                    They'll see the *traigh adhairt*.

dern, hide	twa-neukit, two-horned
bauch, commonplace	scaldachan, chattering

traigh adhairt, landfall

23

Cheepin' and squakin' like a puckle mice
Aneth a firlot! There's a deeper joke
Ahint the *gair nan tonn* than they jalouse
They micht as weel bide in t he Islands whaur
To 'strains o' little meanin'' folk wi' less
Reap corn, or deer come doon to graze wi' sheep,
And fishermen can ha'e the undeemis stars
Like scorlins roond their thowl-pins ilka nicht
Or ony gudge look through his window-bole
Past nettles, dockens, apple-ringie, heather reenge
And think they're on his rizzar bushes there,
And sae they are as weel as onywhaur else!
The sea gies up its deid. It's a' it gies.
Its deid, or livin' – the apprentice deid!

Even as youth's blindness hauds the body dear
And only slowly, slowly, year by year,
The dark thins and the een o' men grow clear,
My hert'll stiffen and rejoice nae mair
In the lost lilac and the lost sea-voices,
Whaup's cry or goose's gansel o' mankind
Nor set toom forms atween the ivory yetts
Nor curtain them wi' *siantan dubha*, tears,
Or Iolaire's, or angels', wings; but haud
The warld a photo o' me as a loon
I canna mind o' haen been at a'
A state I put awa' wi' spung-taed pranks
              Wi' nae precociousness.

A state removed, as 'Little Gooje' yet
Nae doot'll dae awa' wi' a' the stars.

gair nan tonn, sound of the sea	undeemis, countless
scorlins, tangles of seaweed	gudge, stupid fellow
apple-ringie, wood-ruff	rizzar, currant
hauds, holds	gansel, nonsense-talk
toom, empty	yetts, gates
Iolaire's, eagle's	loon, boy

For Nature's like grown men and Wimmen thrang
Wi' hi-spy, smuggle the geg, crawflee, and tig,
Merry-my tanzie, and beds o' Edinburgh.
And politics, religion, and a' men's ploys
Are nocht but new names for the same auld games
What use for Christ to cry to sic-like folk
To leave a' else ahint and follow him?
I'm no' a Christian but I canna say
That Christianity's failed – it's no' been tried,
Yet it's the warst romanticism o' a'
That ettles to be 'classical' again
             Sae lang since Calvary.

There is nae Kirk; we've only poetry left,
Poetry – or golf, or gairdening, or the like!
Weel then! Tak' back the gowpenfu' o' dirt
That took on life a wee while neath your hand
Shatter, unnatural Nature, heedlessly,
Needlessly, anither Design for a Man.

When you see ither – laicher – forms o' life
Oot o' this waesome corpse poorin' in croods
Are you complacent, findin' them at least
Obedient, mair obedient, to your moods?

Or d'you still dream that this chimera, hope,
Man, and 'yont man – 'll be some fine morn's morn?
You'd be a mither? You've conceived sic things?
To wark, then, wumman! Let the bairn be born!

Mak' a reality o' your fondest dream,
Alas, the distance is owre faur, the gap

thrang, busy
hi-spy, smuggle the geg, crawflee, tig, Merry-my-tanzie, beds o' Edinburgh,
children's games
gowpenfu', fistful   laicher, inferior

Owre deep, for you to cross, nae maitter
Hoo keen you are, between your thocht and lap.

Daith is the only fruit you'll manage
In a' your future struggles to reach and pu'.
Aye mair failures, aye coontless creations
To bear – and bury too.

For graves and cradles multiply themsel's
Age follows age upon your road in vain.
The idea flees you, the idea that draws you
Infinitely – only to withdraw again! . . .

The relation o' John Davidson's thocht
To Nietzsche's is mair important
Than a' the drivel about 'Hame, Sweet Hame'
Fower million cretins mant.

And gin we canna thraw off the warld
Let's hear o' nae 'Auld grey Mither, ava'
But o' Middle Torridonian Arkose
            Wi' local breccias,
Or the pillow lavas at Loch Awe . . .

mant, stammer

26

Up to my Eyes in Debt

Up to the een in debt I stand
My haill life built on shiftin' sand
And feel the filthy grip gang grindin'
Into my brain's maist delicate windin'.
And gin a' Thocht at sicna time
Is present to me what's the use?
It's bad eneuch to droon in slime
And no' rive a' Eternity loose
And pu' it doon alang wi' me
Into the foul diurnal sea,
To mak' a bonny pair at last
Wi' starfish, bottles and corks upcast.

The Problems of the Scottish Soul

The problems o' the Scottish soul
Are nocht to Harry Lauder;
I met a lassie in Maybole,
Athikitty, they ca'd her.
I thocht I'd woo her, but aye at the squeak
O' my muckle buits she was aff like a streak
Sae I tried it syne in my stockin' soles,
And dootless I'd ha'e fund her
But I lost my way – nae wonder,
For they were fu' o' holes.

Then fare you weel Athikitty,
I'll try nae mair, says I
It's haurdly for the likes o' me
To plague a wench sae shy.
There's ither pebbles on the beach
But I'll admit – you are a peach.
I could ha'e had you a' the same
But it'd ha' been a darned shame
– For to gang barefit, d'ye no' see,
'Ud ha' been owre barefaced for me!

(Is this Scots humour? Like a poet wha's
No' in the mood and finds ideas and words
Fell lourd and dour that else were licht as birds
My memory in puir, fushionless outlines draws,
Offsettin' Lauder's, and my ain *that* breeds,
A' kinds o't frae Dunbar richt doon to Burns
Till I'm fair hotchin' wi' its coontless turns,
– A routh o' entertainment dowed, that only needs
Yokin' again to Scots, to loup to life;

lourd, heavy   dour, irresponsive
fushionless, dispirited   hotchin', restless
                    loup, leap

28

But still twixt it and me, a smeekit glass,
Hings this hauf-English, winna let me pass,
And mak's my harns wi' reelin' shadows rife,
Faur ayont which, unkent, lie kinds o' fun
That kent 'ud mak' a'ither humours dun.
– O lauchter that in turn becomes the joke
Lead thou me on – alternate fire and smoke!
Lead thou me on – to still mair leadin' on
There is nae goal, for ony goal 'ud be
A lauch to last for a' Eternity
Wi' nocht ootwith itsel' on which to hone
The keener sense that ser's for aye to pit
The stage afore it in a form absurd
Thus feedin' the crescendo still unheard
When utmaist wit's like idiocy void o' wit.
This is the inevitable end – there is nae joke
That mak's the warld or ony aspect o't
A thing to lauch at but itsel' has got
An airgh o' humour like a nickerin' moke;
Lauchter's nae lauchin' maitter – fegs,
The time 'll come, as shair as eggs is eggs
When I myself 'll be as firmly stuck
In some auld rut o' humour as the ruck.

Certes the time 'll come, but no' juist yet!
Is this Scots humour – (This is it! . . .)

(Can I no' think o' Lauder as Beethoven thocht
O' General Abercrombie in Eroica No. 3?
Pince sans rire, I doot I'm thinkin'
Less o' Beethoven then o' Satie
Embryons Desserchés; the ghaist o' the cuttin' machine
'll ser' me for anither Holothurie

airgh, lack   nickerin', snickering
              moke, horse

29

Or for ocht else the trouble wi' me bein'
As I've just said, that I'm aneth the sea,

And canna rise. Fu' mony a doonsin' gen
The dark, unfathomed caves o' ocean bear,
And true appreciation o' Lauder's ane,
Ineffably amusin' – awa doon there!)

The Nature of Life

There is nae limit to the modes in which
The minds o' men the Universe construe
Save that they're only men's – o' a'e wee star
A'e kind o' its life, and o' that kind as few
Men hae't, the product – Prima Facie, then
Scant is the value o' the minds o' men.

My memory is the warld's: a bearded king,
A lovely wumman, and the rest's a dust
O' nations that gaed through me to their daith
What o' the life that's gane that I su'd trust
The life to come? The future like the Past
'll leave a puckle fragments at the last.

A wanton wumman and a shaggy king
Why sud their memory survive the years?
Wimmen as fair and men wi' langer beards
Are as they'd never been. Fact disappears
And leaves a silly fable in its place,
A whirl o' chariots or a whippet race.

Progress? There is nae progress; nor sall be,
The cleverest men aye find out again
For foolish mobs that follow to forget,
As in the Past, the knowledge men ha'e haen
At stented periods frae the dawn o' Time:
And Sisyphus anew begins his climb.

The cleverest men? Or are there cleverer still?
Those nameless wha by ither standards judge
Than knowledge, beauty, length o' beard or aucht
That history uses, and wha winna budge

stented, set   aucht, anything

31

To humour fame or sense – and are they no'
The mightly masses that we ken nocht o'?

Man's destiny is inseparable from the clods
And a' Life's divers shapes Earth inly spurns
As ane wha sees that a' men's thochts are but
Disguises for the a'e reality o' rut . . .

The God I speak o's him wha made
The warld and ither warlds that are
As different frae't as Night frae Day
Or life frae Death
– The God in whom religions centre,
No' Him that lifts unkennable ayont
Creation and Creator baith!

Wha by Divine can think o' nocht but life
Raised to the heichest poo'er, to mair
Than genius is to common-sense,
Mid-day to mirk,
Ettlin' to turn into angels syne
As caterpillars into moths,
May grub in a kirk.

The Gowden Eagle disna stegh itsel'
On sic cocoons; the betterment o' man,
And a' that life is or sall become
Are nocht to *that* God.
But wha' for a' Creation cares nae mair
Nor less, than for a whigmaleerie, tak's a'e step
Alang his endless road.

God the Creator still maun ser'
The mindless fools wha canna . . .

mirk, dusk   ettlin', endeavouring
stegh, stuff   whigmaleerie, trifle

But to see ev'n him as weel as ony man
Can gin he tries
They maun unbig the warld they're pairt o'
And brak' the foond whaur the serpent
As a sacrifice lies,

The immortal serpent wa'd up in life
As God in the thochts o' men.
– Open the grave o' the universe
And it'll loup oot again;
And your een sall be like the Bible syne
Gin its middle was tint
And Genesis and Revelation
Alane left in't
Suddenly my verse 'll gie men
Glisks o' the serpent wallopin'
Wi' a' that they are gien' way afore it
As a nichtmare rides;
Wi' a' that they are turnin' to pairt o't
Like silly shapes that thow in a dream,
Like Athikte here, or the bumbaized warld
The Flood row'd in its tides.

This, at best, is the God that men
Can humanly ken; and the serpent's
The clearest sense o' the nature o' life
To which they can win
– God whirlin' in Juggernaut while under its wheels
The generations are drawn and vanish
Like rouk in the sun!

unbig, unbuild	foond, foundation
wa'd, walled	tint, lost
thow, thaw, melt	Athikte, goddess of measurement
bumbaized, bamboozled	row'd, rolled
rouk, mist	

In the Light of Totality

There's naething that a man can be
That's mair than imbecile to me
In the licht o' totality.

Nae man worth ca'n a man can thole
To be haud'n doon to ony role.
– Fegs! I'm no' browdened on the whole.

Hoo can I sing lest I begink
Mysel' wi' a sang less mine than I think
Or some short-circuit o' a kink?

And what but that is this a'e doot
Still glimmerin' in a warld o' soot?
What else'd I ha'e gin *that* gaed oot?

Where is the Fool?

Whaur is the fool that hasna wished
That he'd been God and no' anither,
And ev'n in daen't thocht o' a'
Frae sicna role micht gar him swither
And kent Go even better by that
Yet ev'n in feelin' he kent Him better
Kent that nae man can think o' God
In terms ayont his ain puir natur'
And syne, in kennin that, kent God
As something he could never ken
And felt his ain life soarin' up
To hidden heichts, like some great Ben?
On sicna heichts I'll big my nest
Soar thence and sing, licht doon and rest,
And whiles see a' the warld as yince
An airman fleein' through the mist
Saw in a rift wi' startled een
A promontory sheep and wist
Hoo dangerously laigh he'd been.
 – *Aye! That's what's ca'd a nose-dive, Prince!*

I wha wad sing as never Scotsman sang afore
(And could owre easily, but in anither sense!)
And yet as naebody but a Scotsman ever will
The tables for my unkent God's communion fence
 – Queerly encuch (tho' a' my braidclaith's nakedness)
Feelin' like ony ordinar' elder, mair or less.

Cette antique union du Poete et du Prêtre . . .

Sheep's face be gane. My spirit canna be mair
Than a distortit memory o' the U.P. Kirk

swither, hesitate   laigh, low
     ca'd, called

As lang as you're aboot. Aye, tho' I ordain,
Wi' layin' on o' hands, and covert smirk,
The whore o' Babylon – or ony ither whore –
To join the Session, it'll be a tethered splore,
Haud'n to the common God like a bird in a cage;
E'en Clootie winna ser' me for he's naething but
God's ain sel' flyped, and apt to richt himsel'
At disconcertin' times – as a silly gut
While hides in a dirl o' music tae
Its intention to brak' in the usual way.

And aye the veil is rent and a' I see
In horror-stricken blasphemy is mysel'
As in a mirror, and owre my shoulder, Daith,
And yon't Daith Life again – an endless swell
O' mountain efter mountain, a faithfu' flock
Each wi' a bawbee for the collection poke!

tethered splore, adventure within prescribed limits
Clootie, the Devil   flyped, turned inside out
bawbee, half-penny   poke, bag

Not Tir-nan-og, but America?

A sideless, bottomless, endless sea
      Is no' for me,
A waesome jobble, nae skyline seen,
Nae land, 'loved mansionry, jutty or frieze,
Or coign o' vantage' that comfort's yin's een
Or a 'procreant cradle' to man's mind gies.
Still less can I thole the silly emotion
That conjures up, confrontin' the ocean,
A Land Under Waves or some sic freak
Like the 'bune-sky Heaven Christians seek.

Folk wi' the sea, wha nae mair ha'e hoped,
      Ha'e never coped.
Their sangs are the sangs o' gulls no' men.
Their Hebrides are like Coleridge's talk
Gien' glisks o' intelligibility, then
The foggy curtain again draps back.
– Wad it had lifted and left bare
The meanin' o' the islands there
While owre the restless gulf folk saw
No' Tir-nan-og, but America!

Unguardit frontier facin' a West
      No' o' the Blest!
It's no' Missus Kennedy Fraser's sangs,
A' verra weel for Sasunnachs and seals,
That'll voice the feelin's movin' amang's
To whom the sicht as to men appeals.
Let's hear nae mair o' Tir-nan-og
Or the British Empire! See the fog
Is liftin' at last, and Scotland's gien,
Nae bletherin' banshee's, but Europe's een.

thole, endure
Mrs Kennedy-Fraser, collector of Hebridean folk songs
varra, very   weel, well

I hear a Fool . . .

I hear a fool (Plotinus he is ca'd)
Say, 'Intelligence was a Unity, but alas
        Didna bide as it was,
But unkent to itsel' turned mony-fa'd,
Grew pregnant . . . Wae for its posterity!
Better there ne'er had been a Secondary!'
And turn to Thocht as wha to a trauchled wife,
Mindit in sair times o' blithe coortin days
        Turns to'r and says:
'Your fond dream little recked o' sic a life.
Yon were the happy days. Wad ye no' lief
Ha'e a' sin-syne undune, wi'ts want and grief?'
And hears her say: 'You think I little kent?
I kent a'richt – and yet was willin',
        And that's the mood I'm still in.'
And little tho' the cratur's life has meant
– Her's and her man's and bairns' a' meanly spent –
I ken that she is richt and a' her pain
And seemin' waste o' effort better than nane
        Tho' I'd fain
Ha'e had her tyauvin' on a different plane
Few folk ha'e ever gained or 'll ever gain,
A number that'd no' be sair increased if a'
The need for ither effort was ta'en awa'
        – As it'll yet be ta'en!

ca'd, called	mony-fa'd, manifold
trauchled, troubled	sair, difficult
sic, such	lief, rather
sin-syne, since then	tyauvin', struggling

Scotland's Purpose

I ken the stars that seem sae faur awa'
Ha'e that appearance juist because my thocht
Canna yet bridge the spiritual gulf atween's
And the time when it will still seems remote
   As interstellar space itsel'
Yet no' sae faur as 'gainst my will I am
Frae nearly a'body else in Scotland here.
But a less distance that I'll drive betwixt
   England and Scotland yet
(Wrang-heidit? Mm. *But heidit! That's the thing.*)

I ken what gars the feck o' folk
Accept the rule o' Fate,
And till last year
Used whiles to fear
A' men, at least in Scotland here,
'Ud gang that thowless gait.

But I ha'e found co-workers syne
In whom I see the licht
O' wills like mine
Increasin' shine
– In a'e shape to unite.

Nae doot in ithers I dinna ken,
Gin I could only see
The spirit's at work
– And it may lurk

wrang-heidit, wrong-headed   gars, makes
feck, majority   whiles, at times
thowless, strengthless   gait, way
      a'e, one

Unkent in neist to a'body
Unkent to a' eternity.

For I've nae hope o' maist folk . . . yet.
The few in whom it shines
'll aiblins multiply
Till by and by
The haill shape, big or sma', defines,

The shape o' Scotland's purpose
Its profitable will,
– Or imitation o't
Due to oor faulty thought,
But wi' its ain pooer still.

(Scotland's purpose to the world's
A comparison to me
As 'twere a bonny dear
To the serpent at her ear
Movin' like the Fir-clisne
              There.)

Sae we maun sing as we were richt
And canna be mista'en
Nor doot by sicna sang
No' Fate but Destiny plain
'll kyth amang's or lang,
And error set Reason ga'en.

As lanely in the croodit streets
We gang, yet here and there
There beeks in Scottish een

neist, next	a'body, everybody
siblins, perhaps	sicna, such-like
kyth, manifest itself	amang's, among us
	beeks, flashes

A licht owre lang unseen,
But what it yet may mean
To Scotland, and to mair
Than Scotland, we're no' shair
And in the meantime needna care
But act as tho' we were . . .

      shair, sure

All That's Eternal Fears Fulfilment

A' that's eternal fears fulfilment. Whiles
I look at Scotland and dumfounded see't
A muckle clod split off frae ither life,
Shapeless, uncanny, unendurable clod
Held in an endless nightmare (like a foetus
Catcht up in a clood) while a voice
Yowls in my lug: 'You'll find nae way oot.
Its spell is no' to brak,' and syne I see
My fellow countrymen as gin they were
The Thing that loups at noon frae nature whiles,
Unshaped but visible, horrible and august,
Blastin' the sicht like a'thing seen at aince,
The Black Mass o' the Scottish people,
                    Like Werfel's *Bocksgesang*.

It's little I care for mysel' or my freens.
My concern's wi' humanity, waefully imperfect
And in peril o' destruction. *That* gars me seek
In the secret pairts o' my spirit and like Dante
Cry oot on the heedless and laggard.
In the shock o' despair, the hopelessness,
The οργασμδς o' liberated hate and lust,
A new element comes into bein' – wider
And stranger than ocht that the clay can ken,
The mysterious meetin' place, where for a flash
Earthly touches divine and wins new strength,
Courage to face past and present that promise
That frae their base frenzies may come even yet
                    Something worth while.

O human thocht that maun aye owrethraw.
A' that it touches, create but to destroy,
Amid the desolation language rises

And towers abune the ruins and music wi't.
Poetry's the movement that the mind invents
For its expression, even as the stars,
And wins to a miraculously calm, assured,
Awareness o' the hidden motives o' man's mind
        Nocht else daur seek.

The Only Road is Endless

The only road is endless. Few ha'e ta'en't.
Sma' as a bawbee is the sphere o' Man.
Gin' the diameter o' ilka coin that's e'er
Been minted's taen and added up and made
The radius o' human life 't'ud be nae odds.
A' but an odd man here and there 'ud bide
Sae close to the centre o't it micht as weel
Be juist a bawbee still or threepenny bit,
As thick as flies upon a plat o' shairn
In simmer – and nane thinks to try the sun.
Gang near them and they'll row your heid in crape,
A black and stinkin' clood that's Hell itsel'.
Leave them to their Aiberdeen and Twal' Mile Roond!

The only road is silence, for nae sang
Has yet been sung and aiblins ne'er will be
That isna haud'n like a fly as weel
To the same plat o' shairn. The only road
Is dark withoot a whistle. There's nae road
Unless we mak' it – gin it can be made,
For nocht's been thocht oot yet and nocht's been planned
And a' humanity has dune's to crood
The puslock in the season and syne breed
Their like to cover it mair blackly yet
Neist season, and the neist, and there's nae end
To the numbers it'll haud at last
        Like angels on a needle's point.

plat o' shairn, lump of shit   **puslock, lump of shit**

Man, the reality that makes all things possible, even himself

Man's the reality that mak's
A' things possible, even himsel',
Energy's his miracle
But hoo little he's dune wi't yet.
Denyin't at ilka turn.
Ilka change has Eternity's mandate.
But hoo little we've changed since Adam,
Frightened to open oor minds,
Frightened to move.
To the foolish a' comes and gangs lichtly
But what can we dae wha's spirits
Unceasingly strew dark on oor days
And pride themsel's on't, makin' life harsh
In oor herts, since a' that's Eternal
                    Fears fulfilment.

But maist poets even follow ane anither
Like sheep through a gap in a dyke
Drawin' 'their' ideas frae a fringe
O' the Kabbala, withoot kennin'
Whaur they come frae or what they mean
And no' fashin' to gang back
To the sources themsels to see
Gin there's no' better anes there untouched
Than the wheen that ha' aye been taen
– No' stoppin' to speir if they wadna
Be better to think for themsels
At this time o' day, no' refurbish
                    Notions o' slaverin' savages,
On which they're borne as I've seen in a spate

wheen, few   speir, question
                    spate, flood

45

Tree-trunks, sheep, bee skeps and the like
    On the bible-black Esk.

Ah, double nature, distinct yet ane,
Like Life and Thocht. For Nature is
A moment and a product o' the Mind,
And no' a Mind that stands abune the warld
Or yet rins through it like a knotless threid
But coincides wi't, ane and diverse at aince;
An eternal solution and eternal problem.
A' things substitute themsel's, ane for the ither.
And everything joins on to everything else,
A tissue o' multiple meanings? Oor myriad symbols
Are the masks o' the Cosmos; and Man's job's
To mak' myriads mair, a new *Imitation*.
Confrontin' the impassive eternal universe
Wi' the states o' his restless hert?
Then what'll I turn to noo, like a loon
Clingin' at Manhood still as to a Noah's Ark
Or cairdboard ferm? Ocht I can ha'e – a'thing –
Is nae mair use to me noo than my mither's womb,
And I've tint my amusement at maitter,
The quick-change artist,
Ashamed o' ha'en a'e form insteed o' anither,
And hastenin' to cheenge it – the haste that is
Its a'e reality – and canna find ocht
Wha's unavoidable annoyance ony langer
May be taen as Apollinaire took
    The War – wi' irony!

The wecht o' water in the ocean and
The immeasurable distances o' the stars
Nae mair annihilate or affect my thocht;
And I can counterbalance mony anither
Blind force o' Nature wi' byordinar ease,

threid, thread   byordinar, exceptional

And yet it's still a multitudinous melee o' forms,
A thrang stream in which beauty is tint
As sune as it kyths; and even as a few men's thocht,
Their fringe o' consciousness and will, is thrawn up
Oot o' the dark and void, perishable and fine
As a hair, wi' its fate still ungaurdit,
– Aye, even as Man roamin' the Earth
For a thousand centuries at last gied birth
To a wheen men learnin' to be prudent and think
Wha's learnin' seemed juist to reverse
The motions that led them to't
Cryin' sympathy, tenderness and the law o' luve,
But the words were nae suner spoken
Than the lips that spoke them were whelmed in the spate
And the braith that made them broke like a bubble
– Sae I, pinnin my faith to Thocht, ken weel
Its accidental character, weakness, and limits
And that a' but a few men trust naethin' sae little
As this poo'er that alane divides – can divide –
Them frae the beasts that perish; frae bees and ants
Wi' their wonderfu' organizations. What has man dune
That I should prefer his arts and ideas
To the hives o' bees or colonies o' ants
   Or think God does?

Santayana and Bruce frae a spider
Learnt different lessons, and there's ithers to learn.
Man's in the makin' but henceforth maun mak' himsel'.
Nature has led him sae faur, up frae the slime,
Gi'en him body and brain – and noo it's for him
To mak' or mar this maikless torso.
Let him look to Nature nae mair;
For her will's to create ane wi' the poo'er
To create himsel' – if he fails, she fails
And the metal gangs back to the pot
  kyths, appears

47

                    And the process
Begins a' owre. If he wins he wins alane.
                    It lies wi' himsel'.

Up frae the slime, that a' but a handfu' o' men
Are grey wi' still. There's nae trace o't in you.
Clear withoot sediment. Day withoot nicht.
A' men's institutions and maist men's thochts
Are tryin' for aye to bring to an end
The insatiable thocht, the beautiful violent will,
The restless spirit of Man, the theme o' my sang
Or to the theme o't what Man's spirit and thocht
Micht be if men were as muckle concerned
Wi' them as they are wi' fitba' or wimmen,
Poets' words as the neist door neighbours'
And if they werena at the mercy
O' the foul mob when they kyth in an antrin man
A property snake to the snake that blends and twists,
Flashing, wise, sinuous, dangerous creature,
Offspring of mystery and the world without end
                    That rises and spreids its hood
                    And leans and listens
                    In ecstasy swaying
Even whaur by the Feshie the sand pipers twitter
And the reid and white foxgloves wag in the wind
Or wha's coils eely awa' like water through sand
Or are like the stags in the Forest o' Gaich
You maun strike on the flanks to wauken
When they'll up and owre the hill-taps
                    Like flashes o' lichtnin'.

Earth's rinnin' doon like a clock;
A' its changes mak' for the final
State o' No Change? In the mighty field

antrin, occasional   Feshie, a Scottish river
                    eely, ebb

Owre which the tide is fleetin'
To leave bare a' meanin' at last
Will some coonter-force suddenly appear?
There's nae sign o't yet, and what if it does
Tellin' a similar story
In anither language and style?
I see your coils twined to a point
Faur ayont Opiuchus (as on Monadh nan Eun
And by mony a green bealach I see
The tragic struggle betwixt
Demoniacal pooers o' beauty
On the a'e hand and on the ither
Truths, quiet and salutary,
Shinin' frae afaur); and a'thing else
A grey skin you've cast, Cencrastus,
Loupin' there oot o' hule; and cry 'Thocht'
Tho' I ken that nae thocht 'll survive
– Nocht at last but a quality o' mind
Committed to nae belief
No' Thocht, but a poo'er to think,
And 'ud fain stake *that* in a Scottish form
       In the endless hazard.
A poo'er to think, no' to be led astray,
Eident and lintwhite and caulder than ice
Takin' a' that you can frae the sun
And gi'en nocht in return, your coils are no'
Mair numerous than the plies o' my brain.
Your scepticism gangs nae deeper.
A single movement shows that Licht
Flows frae nae central source in Heaven
But is a product o' ilka star itsel'.
Syne in a single lirk you haud
Mair darkness than midnicht or men's herts.
Hoo can my mind be ane wi' you

Cencrastus, the snake symbolizing the fundamental pattern of the universe
Eident, clear

To whom Man's fate or Earth's is o' sma' concern?
Hoo can my mind be ane wi' you
Understandin' a' that is and is to be
As weel as men think they ken
Some period o' history and can seize
On the aefauld principle that lay under
A' its divers facts (tho' they canna)?
Yet, if I dinna, I'm a bairn wha thinks
                    The Mune's made o' green cheese!

aefauld, single, opposite of manifold

The Unconscious Goal of History

Unconscious goal of history, dimly seen
In Genius whiles that kens the problem o' its age
And works at it; the mass o' men pursue
Their puir blind purposes unaware o' you,
And yet frae them emerges tae your keen
Clear consequences nae man can gauge
Save in relation to some ancient stage;
Sae History mak's the ambitions o' great men
Means to ends greater than themsels could ken,
– Greater and ither – and mass ignorance yields,
Like corruption o' vegetation in fallow fields,
The conditions o' richer increase; – at last
The confusion's owre the time comes fast
When men wauk to the possibility
O' workin oot and makin' their destiny
In fu' consciousness and cease to muddle through
Wi' nae idea o' their goal – and nae mair grue!

Let nane cry that the right men arena here
– That urgent tasks await that nane can dae.
Times oft mistak' their problems in that way.
At the right time the richt men aye appear.
If Scotland fills us wi' despair we may
Be proposin' a goal that disna lie
Onywhaur in history's plan the noo; we sigh
In vain – because we canna think in vain
And oor desire'll hae its due effect
In the lang run altho'oor age rejects.
But a'e thing's certain – nae genius'll come,
Nae maitter hoo he's shouted for, to recreate
The life and fabric o' a decadent State
That's dune its work, gien its idea to the world,

wauk, waken

The problem is to find in Scotland some
Bricht coil o' you that hasna yet uncurled,
And, hoosoever petty I may be, the fact
That I think Scotland isna dune yet proves
There's something in it that fulfilment's lacked
And my vague hope through a' creation moves.
The Unconscious Ideas that impel a race
Spring frae an ineffable sense o' hoo to be
A certain kind o' human being – Let's face
This fact in Scotland and we'll see
The fantasy o' an unconquerable soul
Neath nations' rivalries, persecutions, wars,
The golden casket o' their Covenant, their goal,
Shrined in a dwelling that ootshines the stars,
A dwelling o' delight no' made wi' hands,
For wha's sake till the gaen oot o' the Sun
They'll hew the Sassenach, the Amalekite, the Hun
Nor sacrifice the least fraction o' their will
To independence while they've a tittle still
O' their Unconscious Idea unrealised.
Is Scotland roupit that I su'd gie owre
My quest for onything, hooso'er disguised,
That wi' a new vitality may endower
My thieveless country: and mak' it mair
Intelligently allied to your hidden purpose there
Sae that my people frae their living graves
May loup and play a pairt in History yet
Wi' sufferin's mair like a Genius's than a slave's,
Vieve strands in your endless glories knit?
By thocht a man mak's his idea a force
Or fact in History's drama: he canna foresee
The transformations and uses o' the course
The dialectics o' human action and interaction 'll gie
The contribution he mak's – it'll a' depend

roupit, bankrupt   thieveless, spiritless
                    Vieve, vivid

On his sincerity and clearness in the end
And his integrity – his unity with you;
Strivin' to gie birth to that idea through
Him wha o' makin' his meanin' clear
May weel despair when you disappear – or appear.
Stir me, Cencrastus. If the faintest gleam
O' you kyths in my work fu' weel I ken
That your neist movement may lowse a supreme
Glory – tho' I'm extinguished then!

If there is ocht in Scotland that's worth ha'en
There is nae distance to which it's unattached
– Nae height, nae depth, nae breadth, and I am fain
To see it frae the hamely and the earthly snatched
And precipitated to what it will be in the end
A' that's ephemeral shorn awa' and rhyme nae mair
Mere politics, personalities, and mundane things,
Nor mistak' ony philosophy's elaborate and subtle form
That canna fit the changed conditions, for your trend
Drawin' a' life's threids thegither there
Nor losin' on the roonaboots, nor gainin' on the swings
But like the hairst that needs baith sun and storm,
Simmer and winter, Life and Daith . . . A' roads are closed:
North, South, East, West nae mair opposed.
Withoot a leg to stand on, like a snake
Wi' impossible lustres I shake
Earth contracts to a single point of licht
As men, deceived by their een, see stars at nicht,
And the religious attitude has found
In Scotland yet a balancin' ground.

The Fundamental Images of the Sea and the Snake

An image o' the sea lies underneath
A' men's imaginations – the sea in which
A' life was born and that cradled us until
We cam' to birth's maturity. Its waves bewitch
Us still or wi' their lure o' peacefu' gleamin'
Or hungrily in storm and darkness streamin'

The imagination has anither poo'er – the snake,
He who beats up the waters into storm
Wha's touch electifies us into action;
In the abyss o' their origin, their basic form,
A' oor imaginations partake
O' ane or th'ither – the sea or the snake.

The twasome control a' the drama o' life
Gin we talk o' love and freedom, and tell
Oor dreams o' order and peace, equality and joy
We are under the blissfu' waters' spell
And oor een and oor voices betray
Oor inspiration in the bricht sea's sway.

Gin we speak o' Imperial Poo'er, Aristocracy,
Authority, Privilege, Control o' the world
The music changes – on a rattle o' drums
We rise to heights o' glory and death: we've unfurled
An oriflamme; in the glitter o' the latest ideas
The auld serpent is a' yin sees.

The words and ideas change: but under them still
The serpent stirs or the sea allures.
We're deceived nae mair: 'neath a' certain plane
Science, art are a' but the ravings
O' th' poo'ers o' th' abyss; men the instrument

O' the water or the serpent.
They strive forever to master the minds o' men
And rule them wi' strange rhythms. Few ken them.
Maist folk gang through life and never see
The marionettes they are – what forces pen them
Subservient to the serpent's magic or
The charmin' o' the sea that has nae shore.

But there are aye a wheen minds in whom
The surgings and writhings cease.
They dismay anger wi' their smile
And o' diverse notions mak' harmonies
Wi' freendly understandin's flashin' speech
Or unexpected tranquilisin wit.

For them there's nae mair sea; the snake
Is chained in the depths o' a bottomless pit
The serene fury o' ha'en seen th' ineffable's theirs
They are absolved frae a' worship and gang
In the strength o' their ain souls – it is they
Wha recreate man's thocht and change his state;
By what are they ken't – for whom nocht prepares?
Only their like 'll no guess wrang
But twa features they hae – whatever they say
Is something that few can believe: and yet
Never the opposite to general belief.
They never come except in due season
And croon a' controversies wi' a reason
Never heard o' before – yont ilka faction
– [*And aye a reason for action*] !

The Stone called Saxagonus

Mrs Kennedy-Fraser's Hebridean songs – the whole
Celtic Twilight business – I abhor,
Just as in Scandinavian music I have no use
For 'the delightful taste of a pink sweet filled with snow'*
The delicate pastel shades, the romantic nostalgia,
Found also in writers like Jens Jacobsen.
Ibsen's hardy intellectual virility is matched
By Sibelius but by hardly anyone else.
Give me Gaelic poets and composers again
Who will stand first and foremost as Sibelius stands,
Towering overwhelmingly over the Palmgrens and Jarnefelts
(Though I do not undervalue the Finnish comic strain
– An element absent from Sibelius's scores –
Found in Palmgren's 'Humorous Dance In The Finnish Style'
Though it only peeps out there, not given breadth
As in Dargomizhsky's 'Finnish Fantasia';
Comicality abounds in the Hebrides too
But our crepuscular 'creators' make nothing of it.) –
For harsh, positive masculinity,
The creative treatment of actuality
– And to blazes with all the sweetie-wives
And colourful confectionery.
The Orpheus Choir, Rev. Kenneth McLeod, and all the rest!
They have bemused the geology of the islands
Till every other stone has become a Saxagonus,
Which stone 'if it be holden against the sun,
Anon it shall shape a rainbow,'
And the rest Gagathes and white margery pearls.
A fit setting only for spooks!†

* Debussy's impression of Grieg's pieces for strings.
† See the description of Ireland in the sixteenth-century Book of Howth, (Cal. of Carew MSS.)

Plaited like the Generations of Men

Come, follow me into the realm of music. Here is the gate
Which separates the earthly from the eternal.
It is not like stepping into a strange country
As we once did. We soon learn to know everything there
And nothing surprises us more. Here
Our wonderment will have no end, and yet
From the very beginning we feel at home.

At first you hear nothing, because everything sounds.
But now you begin to distinguish between them. Listen,
Each star has its rhythm and each world its beat.
The heart of each separate living thing
Beats differently, according to its needs,
And all the beats are in harmony.

Your inner ear grows sharper. Do you hear
Your deep notes and the high notes?
They are immeasurable in space and infinite as to number.
Like ribbons, undreamt-of scales lead from one world to another,
Steadfast and eternally moved.
(More wonderful than those miraculous Isles of Greece
'Lily on lily, that o'erlace the sea,'
Than the marvellous detailed intensity of Chinese life,
Than such a glimpse as once delighted me of the masterly and
    exhaustive

'The gods have placed Vishnu to the East surrounded him with metres (*chandobhir abhitah paryagrihan*); saying "On the south side I surround thee with the Gayatri metre; on the west side I surround thee with the Trishtubh metre; on the north I surround thee with the Jagati." Having thus surrounded him with metres, they placed Agni on the east, and thus they went on worshipping and toiling. By this means they acquired this whole earth (*tena imam sarvam prithivim samvindata*.' – Satapatha-brahmana 'When we have once penetrated the vaults of Nature's mysterious palace we can learn to speed our soul with the wings of speech, and it will chime away in ever more blossoming and sublime melody.' (With acknowledgements to Ferrucio Busoni.)

57

Classification of psychical penetrations and enlacements
On which Von Hartman relied, giving here some slight
   dissection
Of the antinomies underlying ethical thought, discussing
   there the gradations
Of the virtues, the stratifications of axiology, with an
   elaborate power
And beauty – but there! – Oh, Aodhagan O Rathaille meets again*
The Brightness of Brightness in a lonely glen
And sees the hair that's plaited†
Like the generations of men!)

All the knowledge is woven in neatly
So that the plaited ends come to the hand.
Pull any of the tabs, and a sequence
Of practical information is drawn.

Each sound is the centre of endless circles,
And now the *harmony* opens out before you.
Innumerable are its voices, compared with which
The boom of the harp is a screeching,
The clash of a thousand trumpets a twitter.

* Aodhagan O Rathaille, Irish Gaelic poet, 1670–1726. The reference is to O'Rahilly's great *aisling* (i.e. vision poem), '*Gile na Gile*.'

† See also the third section of Professor R. B. Onians' *The Origin of European Thought* (London 1952), which is concerned chiefly with words connected with fate which can be interpreted as terms connected with spinning and weaving and the use of their product. The word *peirar*, often translated 'end', means a bond or cord which the gods can put on a person or an army (and Ocean is the bond round the Earth, although here the bond is slipping over into the meaning of boundary and so end); the image of binding is often used to express the power of fate or the gods over men, and if we ask what these cords are with which fate binds men, Professor Onians answers that they are the threads which fate or the gods have spun, and that in certain phrases fate itself is thought of as a thread or bond which is put upon men. A further very important chapter deals with *telos*. *Telos* (which means 'end' in the later Greek) in Homer 'covers a man's eyes and nostrils, and so seems also to be some sort of bond'. *Peirar* even in Homer already has the abstract meaning of boundary, but the boundary is doubtless still felt as a physical rope. See also Professor Onians' remarks on the words *thymos, psyche, moirai, phren* and *noos*.

All, all the melodies hitherto heard and unheard
Ring out in full number together, bear you along,
Crowd over you, sweep past you – melodies of love and passion,
Of the Spring and the Winter, of melancholy and abandon –
And they themselves are the spirits
Of a million beings in a million ages
Revealed as Krishna revealed his form

In the Udyoga-parva of the Maha-bharata
Or like the vision of the Universal Form (visva-rupa darsanam)
Before which Arjuna bowed with every hair on his body
    bristling with awe
(Or like the tremendous vision
Which came to Buddha under the Bo-Tree*
Or to Socrates when he heard or dreamt he heard,
The Sybil of Mantinaea
Discoursing on mortal and immortal love
Or like Descartes' dream of November 10, 1619,†
Near the environs of Ulm
When there were presented to him,
Coming as an enquirer after truth,
A Dictionary, representing knowledge,
And the volume of the Corpus Poetarum,
Which he took to be the symbol of inspiration,
Or like the 'sudden illumination' that came
To Benchara Branford one night in his fortieth year:
'At once was born into vivid and enchanting consciousness
A new metaphysical calculus of sixty-four
Inter-related cardinal categories, of which thirty-six
Were the transmuted forms of the Geddesian concepts.'‡
Or like the moment (not like it – it!)
By which as Kierkegaard says in *Begrebet Angst*
The individual is related to eternity,

* In the Bhagavad-Gita. Compare also Matthew XVII, 6, and Luke V, 8.
† Chevalier, *Vie de Descartes*, pp. 40–47.
‡ i.e. The concepts of the late Sir Patrick Geddes, Branford's collaborator.

The moment St Paul refers to when he describes
Our all being changed 'in the twinkling of an eye'
Because in that moment the individual chooses himself
And thereby all may be changed.
The moment partakes of eternity:
It is then eternity penetrating time.
How the moment can be made eternity
For the individual Kierkegaard shows
In 'Gjentagelsen' – depends on repetition,

Kierkegaard's substitute for Plato's theory of reminiscence.)
If you examine one of them more closely you will see
How it clings together with the others, is conjoined with them,
Coloured by all the shades of sound, accompanied
By all the harmonies to the foundation of foundations in the depths
And to the dome of all domes in the heights.

Now you understand how stars and hearts are with another
And how there can nowhere be an end, nowhere a hindrance;
How the boundless dwells perfect and undivided in the spirit,

How each part can be at once infinitely great and infinitely small,
How the utmost extension is but a point, and how
Light, harmony, movement, power
All identical, all separate, and all united are life.

Svaham aham samharami*

Or like that moment in which Kassner assembles
The scattered fragments of his personality
By identifying a strain of music
Heard through the walls of his cell
With the struggle of his comrades thoughout the world
In the same cause.†

* I myself will again bind the braid together. (See Bhattana-rayana's well-known
drama *Veni-samhara*, i.e. 'braid-binding.')
† *Vide* 'Days of Wrath,' by André Malraux.

'Kassner, shaken by the song,
Felt himself reeling like a broken skeleton.
These voices called forth relentlessly
The memory of revolutionary songs
Rising from a hundred throats,
Their tunes scattered and then picked up again by the crowds
Like the rippling gusts of wind over fields of wheat
Stretched out to the far horizon.
But already the imperious gravity of a new song
Seemed once more to absorb everything into an immense slumber;
And in this calm, the music at last rose above its own heroic call
As it rises above everything
With its intertwined flames that soothe as they consume,
Night fell on the universe,
Night in which men feel their kinship on the march
Or in the vast silence,
The drifting night, full of stars and friendship.'

Or is this, albeit language
Infected by positive vision,
Until, like that of Marlowe and the early Elizabethans,
It takes on vigorous new rhythms
And a fresh accretion of savagery,
Subject still to all the objections
Commonly raised against rhetoric?
– The reflection of ideas and values
Not yet wholly assimilated by the sensibility,
So that I seem to be resolving my conflicts
By a kind of verbal self-hypnosis
– Communicating an excitement that resides
Too much in a certain use of language
And too little in the ordering of materials?
Am I only fobbing myself off
With a few more of those opiate-like phrases
Whose repetition so readily operates
As a substitute for discovery –

Instead of realizing the concept
Of an ultimate metaphysical scheme
Under which we have to suppose
A triadic movement of the Universe
In the course of which
We can think of the continuous
As having existed without a beginning
And of its coming to a close,
So that the discontinuous may safely begin
. . . And of the discontinuous coming to a dead end
As it is bound to do
And the continuous reappearing
So that it may continue for ever
And never end?

Have I failed in my braid-binding
At this great crisis
When the impending task of mankind
Is to help to bring to a close the 'conflict' stage
Of the present process of the discontinuous
And to usher in the 'harmony' stage
By means of an abandonment
Of the interlocking and proselytizing technique
Of 'Warfare' and 'persuasion'?
At this moment when braid-binding as never before,
The creation of the seamless garment,
Is the poet's task?

(Even so we have seen a collection of papers
Seemingly multifarious nevertheless connected with a system
As well as entwined together
By their own μέρνις φμεινή
Yet, since the silver cord is often
Intricately knotted in a delicate disorder,*

* 'The warp seemed necessity; and here, thought I, with my own hand I ply my own
shuttle, and weave my own destiny into these unalterable threads.' – Herman Melville,
Moby Dick.

One need not apologize for defining
The author's purpose as embodying
'The doctrine that factors in our experience
Are clear and distinct
In proportion to their variability,'
That 'philosophical truth is to be sought
In the presuppositions of language
And is for this reason akin to poetry.'

And that 'rationalization is the partial fulfilment
Of the ideal to recover concrete reality
Within the disjunction of abstraction.'
– And yet it is none too easy to satisfy oneself
As to the role maximalized 'civilisation' can play
And however resolutely we try to speak
The language of pure metaphysics
We find ourselves wondering
Whether the apotheosis of successful appetition,
Concrete and transcognitive as it may be,
Will not present an ultimate aestheticism
Little less exclusive
Than the intellectualism of Plato.)

The spiritual evolution from vile humanity
To authentic manhood and onward
To participation in self-universal
Is an operation which bases itself
On a full realization of the transiency
Of spatial and temporal conditions,
A permeability of spirit
To those mouldings from the unconscious
Abstractable from such conditions,
An appreciation of the fiduciary status
Of the self, And an ultimate capacity
For transforming the substance of these intuitions
From speculative belief to realized experience.

63

But what proportion of men likely to be saved?
I do not agree that contempt of the simple-minded
Is a limitation that is destructive
Of any poise of the spirit.
Self learns that others in their vileness
(Even those Hollywood moguls for whom
Books are only 'story properties'
Or Horace Tograth, the Australian chemist
Who led the world-wide pogrom against poets
Or Mr Furber, the Canadian dilettante
And all yahoos and *intellectuals-flics*)
Are not subjects for persuasion and alms
But are the appointed task
By which self is to achieve its destiny.
Is this a claim on the part of the self
Of my self – to feel itself superior to other selves?
Even if it is not, the element of rigoristic intellectualism
Present in my message goes beyond
That discoverable in Kant
Who was at least imbued with a conviction
Of the immorality of the idea
That oneself can ever be viewed
As metaphysically distinguishable in status
From another. Well. We have no means
Of deciding whether others are selves
And, if they are, the sort
That consists with self-universal.

Everlasting layers
Of ideas, images, feelings
Have fallen upon my brain
Softly as light.
Each succession has seemed to bury
All that went before.
And yet, in reality,
Not one has been extinguished . . .

The fleeting accidents of a man's life
And its external shows may indeed
Be irrelate and incongruous,
But the organizing principles
Which fuse into harmony,
And gather about fixed pre-determined centres,
Whatever heterogeneous elements
Life may have accumulated from without,
Will not permit the grandeur
Of human unity to be greatly violated,
Or its ultimate repose to be troubled,
In the retrospect from dying moments,
Or from other great convulsions.
It is with me now, surveying all life
From the heights of Literature and the Arts, as it was
With Thomas de Quincey* when he made
A symbology of the view he commanded
From the eminence of Everton.
Liverpool represented the earth,
With its sorrows and its graves left behind,
'Yet not out of sight nor wholly forgotten.'
The moving sea typified the mind.
Here was a respite, the tumult in suspense,
Here, cried de Quincey,
Are the hopes which blossom in the paths of life
Reconciled with the peace which is in the grave;
Motions of the intellect as unwearied as the heavens,
Yet for all anxieties a halcyon calm;
Tranquillity that seems no product of inertia
But as if resulting
From mighty and equal antagonisms,
Infinite activities, infinite repose.
(Even so am I now transformed on this plane
Into the semblance of those who in lower life
Deeming all philosophical systems heretical

* *Vide* Thomas de Quincey's *Suspiria.*

Because they confuse the grammar of human expression
In language, logic, or moral estimation
With the substantial structure of things,
Finding the 'human orthodoxy' round which these heresies play
'The current imagination and good sense of men'
'This orthodoxy is largely erroneous, of course,
But it is capable of correcting its own errors,'
While Heresy is perverse, a 'rebellious partisanship
A deliberate attachment to something
The evidence against which is public and obvious;
It is a sin against the light,'
Springing from 'dominance of the foreground',
The attempt to use as the universal criterion of reality
Some immediate, obtrusive, and familiar aspect of experience
And proclaiming that the true philosopher who is content
To substitute the pursuit of sincerity for the pursuit of
     omniscience
Will not, with the Pragmatists, ignore everything
But utility in relation to human affairs;
Or with the Behaviourists deny the fact of consciousness;
Or with some Idealists deny everything but consciousness;
Or, with other Idealists, everything except logic;
Or, with the New Realists,
Ignore substance and the essences which characterize it,
Or, like Croce, pretend that art is sheer expression,
Imagine that aesthetic experience
Discovers a peculiar kind of good,
In the estimation of which
All other interests are irrelevant.
– Forgetting that every genuine advance in 'human orthodoxy',
Must at first seem only a new heresy
To the blindly orthodox, and that 'human orthodoxy',
May be in some important respect
Quite radically false,
Its correction involving concentration
On some unobtrusive but deeply significant set of facts

Ignored by the orthodox;
And facing at last the possibility
That nature may be but imperfectly formed
In the bosom of chaos, and reason in us
Imperfectly adapted to the understanding of nature.
Yet discovering the secret of peace though bereft
Of Spinoza's consolation – the bare rationality of the universe –
In the fact that mere existence is itself a miracle,
The spirit finds itself 'in the hands
Of some alien and inscrutable power',
And, though that power may be destined to overwhelm us,
'It cannot destroy the joy we had
In its greatness and in its victory;'
This joy of contemplation being one of the most important
And radical of religious perceptions?
(But it conflicts with our felt love
Of the creatures within the universe,
Each of which is seen to be striving
For its peculiar perfection,
'To love things as they are
Would be a mockery of things:
A true lover must love them
As they would wish to be')
Being in short as where literary art
Overpowers philosophical precision
And finding no intellectual solution
For this notorious conflict
Between the 'intellectual love' of the universe as it is
And the moral will that it should be other,
Concluding that perhaps the only solution
Lies in the faith, or the mystical perception,
That the welter of frustration in the parts
Is instrumental to some loftier perfection
In the universe as a whole?

Ah! no, no! Intolerable end
To one who set out to be independent of faith
And of mystical perception.
It does not after all seem certain
That the peace I have found is entirely
Free from mystical elements. Have I found
No salvation but only Santayana again?*
Only *la plus funeste escroquerie à la paix!*
A universal Munich!

Ah, Joyce, not a word, not a word!
I speak to you as if you are still alive.
Alive?
Your memory and your work will live
As long as there are men of letters in the world
And if your grave was here where I stand
(Equally far from all the world
That likes to imagine itself important!)
And I looking at the little hump of it
Through a *claire voie* of iron spikes

---

* M. Paul Hazard in *La Crise De La Conscience Europienne* asks *Qu'est-ce que l'Europe?*
Une pensée qui ne se contente jamais. The Western peoples are immediately distinguished
by a restless activity of mind, by boundless curiosity and insatiable idealism. M. Hazard
does not assert that stability, certitude, serenity are qualities or states completely alien
to the European genius; but he suggests that they are only attained by a sort of paradox,
and that they offer a temptation to fall out in the march, to desist from that perpetual
exploration which is the *dura lex, sed lex* of Europe. If Europe can accept Matisse and
Picasso as great painters, in spite of the extensive break they have made with previous
tradition, there is little reason why Indian art, also, should not come to be more widely
recognized for its actual achievements; although such recognition does involve not merely
a revision of purely aesthetic canons but also an acceptance as legitimate of an outlook on
life, on the status of man and woman in the natural world, which is quite different from
anything that has existed in Europe. That does not mean that Europeans and Indians
need give their approval to everything that has occurred in the past, either in Europe or
India. It means that we should prepare to share in feelings which are not those now
current or those that have ever been current in our own civilizations. Aubrey Menen
says in his *Rama Retold:* 'There comes a time in the history of *every* civilization when,
for the sake of human dignity, men turn their backs on it.'

I would be realizing clearer than ever
– And knowing how greatly that's due to you –
That we are beginning more and more
To see behind, or through, things to something they hide,
For the most part cunningly,
With their outward appearance,
Hoodwinking man with a façade
Quite different from what it actually covers.
– An old story from the point of view of physics.
We know to-day what heat, sound, and weight are,
Or at least we have a second interpretation,
The scientific one. But I know now
Behind this there is another and many more.
But this second interpretation has powerfully transformed
The human mind and caused the greatest type-change
In our history so far – literature in its own way
Must pursue the same course, the trail you blazed.

To-day we are breaking up the chaste
Ever-deceptive phenomena of Nature
And reassembling them according to our will.
We look through matter and the day is not far off
When we shall be able to cleave
Through her oscillating mass as if it were air.
Matter is something which man still, at most,
Tolerates but does not recognize.

'After all, what do we know of this terrible "matter",
    except as a name for the unknown and hypothetical cause
    of states of our own consciousness?'*

And I know with Christian Morgenstern†
That the time will come soon when we will write

* With acknowledgment to Franz Marc (1880-1916).

† Christian Morgenstern: Stufen. *EineEntwickluug in Aphorismen und Tagebuchnotizen* (Munich: Piper Verlag) 1951.

'From beyond'. I mean about much the same things
As always. But whose peculiar fascination now
Will be made transparent.
They will be characterized with entire belief
In their reality. Yet they will have
The effect of hallucinations. They will hold us
Spell-bound like some of the themes of poetry
As we have known it hitherto
But the awe experienced by him
For whom the old world has collapsed
(The change which takes place is not, in fact
An abandonment of belief seriously held
And firmly planted in the mind,
But a gradual recognition of the truth
That you never really held it.
The old husk drops off
Because it has long been withered
And you discover that beneath it
Is a sound and vigorous growth –)
Will be expressed in their portrayal too,
So that they will at once entertain
And excite a profound uncanny wonder,
Falling athwart
The tideless certainty of our disinterestedness.

All but an infinitesimal percentage of mankind
Have no use whatever for versatility and myriad-mindedness;
Erudition means less than nothing to them.
('Larvae, hallucinated automata, bobbins,
Savage robots, appropriate dummies,
The fascinating imbecility of the creaking men-machines,
Set in a pattern as circumscribed and complete
As a theory of Euclid – essays in a new human mathematic.)
Yet, as Gaudapada says, even as a bed,
Which is an assembly of frame, mattress, bedding and pillows,
Is for another's use, not for its own,

70

And its several component parts render no mutual service,
Thence it is concluded that there is a man who sleeps upon the bed
And for whose sake it was made; so this world
Of words, thoughts, memories, scientific facts, literary arts
Is for another's use. Ah Joyce, enough said, enough said!
Mum's the word now! Mum's the word!
Responsibility for the present state of the world
And for its development for better or worse
Lies with every single individual;
Freedom is only really possible
In proportion as all are free.
Knowledge and, indeed, adoption (*Aneignung*)
Of the rich Western tradition
And all the wisdom of the East as well
Is the indispensable condition for any progress;
World-history and world-philosophy
Are only now beginning to dawn;
Whatever tribulations may yet be in store for men
Pessimism is false. Let us make ourselves at home
In *das Umgreifende* the super-objective,
The final reality to which human life can attain.
Short of that every man is guilty,
Living only the immediate life,
Without memory, without plan, without mastery,
The very definition of vulgarity;
Guilty of a dereliction of duty,
The 'distraction' of Pascal,
The 'aesthetic stage' of Kierkegaard,
The 'inauthentic life' of Heidegger,
The 'alienation' of Marx,
The self-deception (*mauvaise foi*) of Sartre.

I believe it will be in every connection soon
As already in the field of colour
Where the imitative stage
Has long been passed

And the coal tar dyes are synthesized no more
To imitate the colours of nature
Whether of Autumn or Spring.
The pattern cards of dye-stuffs firms to-day
Display multitudes of syntheses
That transcend Nature to reach
Almost a philosophic satisfaction
Of the aesthetic sense of colour.
Apart from a handful of scientists and poets
Hardly anybody is aware of it yet.
(A society of people without a voice for the consciousness
That is slowly growing within them)
Nevertheless everywhere among the great masses of mankind
With every hour it is growing and emerging,
Like a mango tree under a cloth,
Stirring the dull cloth,
Sending out tentacles.
– It's not something that can be stopped
By sticking it away in a zinc-lined box
Like a tube of radium,
As most people hope,
Calling all who approve of it mad
The term they always apply
To anyone who tries to make them think.

For Schoenberg was right. The problem involved
In mental vocalization
Is not that the evolution of music
Must wait on the human ear
But that the human ear must catch up
With the evolution of music.
As with Schoenberg's so with your work,
And scant though the evidence be
Of progress here we have ample proof
(While yet the vast majority of mankind
Are but inching to close the infinite gap

And may succeed in a few billion years perhaps)
That the complicated is Nature's climax of rightness
And the simple at a discount. The Apocrypha is right
Of our Muse. 'She needs no simple man'.
We have learned the lesson of the Caddoan saying:
'When a woman grinds the corn with one hand
Don't let it in your belly.'
As in the clash between Red Indian and white man
Sophistication wars with simplicity everywhere
With only one possible conclusion. There can be no doubt
That the bed of which I have spoken will be filled,
All life's million conflicting interests and relationships,
Even as nerves before ever they function
Grow where they *will* be wanted; levers laid down in gristle
Become bone when wanted for the heavier pull
Of muscles which *will* clothe them; lungs, solid glands,
Yet arranged to hollow out at a few minutes' notice
When the necessary air shall enter; limb-buds
Futile at their appearing, yet deliberating appearing
In order to become limbs in readiness
For an existence where they *will* be all-important;
A pseudo-aquatic parasite, voiceless as a fish,
Yet containing within itself an instrument of voice
Against the time when it *will* talk;
Organs of skin, ear, eye, nose, tongue,
Superfluous all of them in the watery dark
Where formed – yet each unhaltingly preparing
To enter a daylight, airy, object-full manifold world
They *will* be wanted to report on. Everywhere we find
Projective knowledge of needs of life
Which are not yet but are foreknown.
All is provided. As Aristotle says,
'To know the end of a thing is to know the why of it.'
So with your work, vastly outrunning present needs
With its immense complication, its erudition,
(The intricacy of the connections defies description.

Before it the mind halts, abased. *In tenuis labor*)
But providing for the developments to come. . . .

Even so long before the foetus
Can have either sensation or motion,
When, in fact, its cellular elements
First begin to differentiate themselves,
The various nerves which are to govern
The perceptions and reactions essential to life
Develop, as they shape themselves, a faculty
For discovering and joining with their 'opposite numbers',
Sensory cell 'calling' to motor cell
By a force we may call Cytoclesis.
Nor is this mysterious 'call'
A phenomenon of the nervous system only.
Throughout the body cell 'calls' to cell
That the elaborate and intricate development
Of tissues may proceed aright.
Thus in the case of the kidney tubules
The myriad secreting tubules are formed
In one portion of the primordial embryonic tissue
Budded out from the ureter.
Nevertheless although these two entities
Are involved in the completion of all the kidney tubules,
There is the marvel that results in each secreting tubule
Meeting a collecting tubule
Accurately end to end.
Each complete duct is composed of two sections
Preformed from different embryological elements
But guided to meet each other by a 'call',
A 'call' so wonderful that each kidney tubule
Meets each ureteric tubule end to end
And so completes the canal.

Ah, Joyce! We may stand in the hush of your death-chamber
With its down-drawn blind

74

But those who were on the other side
When you passed over would find
It (despite the general view: 'Another queer bird gone')
As when – no! Not the Metaphysical Buzzard!
C'est un numéro! C'est marrant – in both senses!)
But the peacock flew in through the open window
With its five-foot tail streaming out behind,
A magnificent *ek-stasis**
Counterpart of your *aufhebung* here,
Der-Sinn des Schaffens† completely seen at last.
– The supreme reality is visible to the mind *alone*.

And so I come to the end of this poem
And bid you, Joyce – what is the word
They have in Peru for *adios?* – *Chau* that's it!
              Well, Chau for now.
Which, as I remember it, reminds me too
Of how in Chile they use the word *roto*
To mean a peasant, a poor man,
In Guatemala called *descalzado*;

And how a man will leave an impression
By the way he mushes his 'r's'
Or buzzes his 'y's' or swallows his 'd's'
So that you automatically think
'Guatemala' or 'Argentina' or 'Colombia'.
They say *bue-no* in Mexico
When they answer the phone.
You can tell a Mexican every time
If you hear him using a phone.
And in Guatemala they use *vos* instead of *tu*

---

* Breaking through to eternity
† The meaning of the Creative Act.

As they would say *che* in Argentina.
And so like Horace long ago,
'*Non me rebus conjugere conor!*'*
Sab thik chha.

---

* Which the Hungarian novelist, Lajos Zilahy, glosses: 'I won't let things get the better of me.' The final (Gurkhali) sentence means 'Everything's O.K.' This indicates that the author shares Werner Bergengruen's conviction of what the German writer calls 'the rightness of the world', despite all that may seem to enforce the opposite conclusion.

The Wrong that is as One with England's Name

'The wrong that is as one with England's name,
Tyranny with boast of liberty, and shame
With boast of righteousness.'
      FRANCIS ADAMS: *Songs of the Army of the Night.*

How much knowledge of imaginative literature*
Does it need to make a proper man?
It used to be said that a proper man was one
Who had built a house, planted a tree,
Begotten a son, and written a book,
And something else . . . played in a county cricket match, perhaps!

At any rate the implication was
That a civilized human being should devote a fifth

---

* 'Our attitude to the literature of the past is almost invariably a kind of genteel idolatry. Instead of asking questions of our great writers we approach them with pious irrelevancy that makes our reading of their works resemble a tourist's pilgrimage to Stratford-on-Avon. Their books lie on our shelves, to be respectfully neglected as so many cultural household gods, or invoked as totems to ward off the onslaught of history. We retire into the cosy warmth of Trollope's England or throw ourselves on the flat bosom of Aunt Betsey Trotwood to get away from the horrors of our day and age. At its best this kind of literary appreciation results in the sort of critical biography at which English men of letters excel. At its worst it leads to the arch parlour-game that we all know so well – the analysis of Branwell Brontë's influence on Charlotte, the discussion of the comparative merits of Jane Austen's heroines . . . . There is something almost indecent about the way in which we rediscover our great writers, remembering them in their centenary years, recalling their eccentricity and charm, their picture in the National Portrait Gallery, their niche in the columbarium of genius. The French rediscover their great writers all the time, but with them such rediscovery is a living intellectual process, a continual restatement of the moral 'Great Debate' which has to be fought out in each generation. . . . Since I first read it, I have been haunted by a kind of parable in M. Sartre's *What Is Literature?* which I think expresses the peculiar danger facing English literary criticism today. 'It must be borne in mind that most critics are men who have not had much luck and who, just about the time they were growing desperate, found a quiet little job as cemetery watchman. . . .' John Raymond on the B.B.C. Third Programme.

Of his time and thoughts to the arts and the humaner letters.
That is more than enough
If the studies are pursued with intelligence,
Eternity will be insufficient to civilize us
If we pursue our slipshod courses.

In the plastic arts, in music, in all foreign literatures
There are artists one calls axioms
... Not because they were supremely great by temperament,
But because they worked supremely
Along one or other technical line.
You may not like Whistler, but you have to accept him
As a prototype of a form of art.
You may not like Jan Van Eyck, Dürer,
Holbein, Velasquez, Rubens, Rembrandt,
Ghirlandaio, Praxiteles, or even Raphael,
But you cannot ignore them
Even should Hokusai be your own master.
Similarly you may not like but cannot ignore
Bach and Palestrina.
It is the same, so far as all but the English
Are concerned, with literature.

No Frenchman can ignore, not the temperaments
But the technical skill,
Of Chateaubriand, Racine, Villon, Gautier,
Musset, Maupassant, Flaubert, and a great
Many other writers from Mallarmé back to Ronsard.
Indeed no human being can afford to ignore them.
... Or Heine, Goethe, Leopardi, Lope de Vega, Turgenev,
Chekhov, Dante, Bertran de Born, Boccaccio,
Catullus, Petronius Arbiter, Apuleius and many more.
To be ignorant – to be utterly ignorant –
Of the methods of any one of these writers
Is to be that extent ignorant
Of some of the ways by which humanity

Can be approached, cajoled, enlightened,
Or moulded into races,
To know all the writings of Heine
Is not necessary, but not to know
How Heine mixed, alternated, or employed
Flippancies and sentiment is to have a blind spot
In your knowledge of how
A part of humanity may be appealed to.

Who among English writers is thus axiomatic?
Accepted thus by either the Anglo-Saxon
Or the foreigner of some culture?
You will say in your haste:
'But there are *hundreds*!
After cursory reflection you will say:
'*But* . . . there are none.'

The name of Shakespeare jumps at once to the lips
But when it comes to the methods of Shakespeare
We know nothing about them
And it is to be doubted
If the Germans know more.
And no other name at all jumps
Or comes ever so reluctantly to the lips.

Why should our Government never think
Of spreading broadcast amongst our men in the Forces
The works of Dickens, Thackeray, Tennyson,
. . . Or even those of Shakespeare?
Why do we not think it essential
That our lawyers and medical men
Should know the works of Meredith at least,
If not those of Henry James?
You will answer it is because Anglo-Saxondom
. . . And a very good thing, too, you will interject . . .
Has never suffered its Governments

To interfere with the arts.
But that is not the answer.

The Foreigner sees or feels that the national arts
Are a product of the national voice
And no Government on the continent of Europe
Can subsist without
Paying some attention to that voice.
So the German State makes axioms of Schiller and Goethe;
The French Republic produces the plays
Of Racine and Molière; Italy
Honours Dante, Tasso, and Petrarch
Whenever it has an opportunity.

We are accustomed to be told
That Anglo-Saxondom would not tolerate
Government interference with the arts;
That it would depose its kings,
Refuse to elect its presidents,
Revolt, erect barricades,
If the State had theatres in which Shakespeare,
Congreve, Vanbrugh, Robertson, and, say, Goethe
Were honoured by classical-minded renderings!

But Anglo-Saxondom wouldn't; Anglo-Saxondom
Does not know that it has any arts;
Does not even know
That play-writing is an art.
If we did know we had arts and neglected them,
Or that the State neglected them,
We might, we should, revolt,
Refuse to pay our taxes
As did the Paris grocers, drink-shop keepers,
Paviors, and municipal slaughterers,
When the French Government tried to economize
By cutting down the subsidy to the Opera.

But the arts, and particularly the written arts,
Of Great Britain have been forced
By the 'highly refined imaginations
Of the more select classes',*
Have been so forced out of all contact with
Or inspiration from the masses
That, inasmuch as any human manifestation
That is taken in hand by any coterie
Or Class of the More Select
Must speedily die,
So literature in Anglo-Saxondom
Has, after growing
More and more provincial, died.
That is not to say that no one
Who writes to-day can write;
It means that the best writers of to-day
Can find only a handful of readers apiece
In the United States;†

And only one handful for all the lot of them
In the British Empire . . . say 14,000
The populations of the British Empire and the United States

---

* Shelley: Preface to 'Prometheus Unbound.'

† '. . . . the consummate diligence with which the moderns – the Anglo-Saxons, in particular – have ignored the strictly poetical works of the still living great of the slightly older generation. It is perhaps safe to say that comparatively few of Thomas Hardy's admirers really understand how much finer is *The Dynasts* than, say, *Tess of the D'Urbevilles*, or even *Jude the Obscure*. But a worse destiny has overtaken the great poets of foreign nations who have outlived their generation. If they are known at all to the English-speaking peoples, it is by their prose or dramatic works; their poetry is hardly read at all. Thus we know d'Annunzio chiefly as the author of *Il Fuoco*, the most unforgivably swinish novel ever written; Verner von Heidenstam by his *Folkungstradet*, Rainer Maria Rilke by a treatise on Rodin, Hugo von Hofmannsthal by the libretto of *Der Rosenkavalier*, and William Butler Yeats by his discourtesy. Of Kostes Palamas, Endre Ady, Ruben Dario, Amado Nervo, Otakar Brezina, Alexander Blok, Holger Drachmann, Antonio Machado, and a dozen other fine spirits, still living or but recently dead, we know, so to speak, little more than their names and quarterings.'

William A. Drake, *Contemporary European Writers.*

Are, say three hundred millions; thus,
Mathematically put, the fraction of readers
For the best work to-day is:

$$\frac{14,000}{300,000,000}$$

It means that in each 100,000 souls
Five are reasonably civilized.

So our literature cannot be called
A very national or even racial affair.
Yet every inhabitant of Athens,
Slaves, helots, and all, must
In the age of Pericles, have had
At least a nodding acquaintance
With the works of Sophocles, Euripides or Pheidias.
Every one of them!

Literature of the imagination in Anglo-Saxondom then
Is not a very thriving national affair
Because it has lost touch completely
With racial life.

To distinctly English writers in England
Authenticity is never allowed;
The quality is perhaps
Not even known to exist.
There are too many vested interests.
In the Unites States Mark Twain
Could finally make headway
Against the Transcendentalists;
Poe could stand with his body starved
But his mind making its mark.
He had to fight many battles
Against many unscrupulous cliques,
And in the end his head became

Both bloody and bowed
But neither he, alive
Nor his reputation, he dead,
Have had to contend with the dead weight
Of dead, vested interests
And merely political disingenuousnesses
That have strangled
Most literary brightnesses
In England for a hundred years.

These tendencies work
Towards a wilderness of thumbs down.
It was Landor who first said
That every Frenchman takes a personal share
In the glory of his poets
Whereas every Englishman resents
The achievements of his poets
Because they detract
From the success of his own 'poetry';
And the remark was extraordinarily profound.
So the English literary world
Is an immense arena
Where every spectator is intent
On the deaths of those awaiting judgement
And every gladiator is intent
On causing the death of his fellow-combatant
By smiting him with the corpses
Of other predeceased.
The method, the mania, the typical
'Fair-play' of 'the sporting English'
Is really extraordinary in its operation.

Supposing, having no pet author of your own
Out of whose entrails
You hope to make a living,
No political bias,

No interest in a firm of publishers
Who make dividends out of other 'classics'
You timidly venture to remark
That Trollope, Jane Austen,
And the Mrs Gaskell of Mary Barton,
Are English Authors
Authentic in their methods.

But you hear the professional reviewers
All protesting at once
'Trollope has not the humour of Dickens,
The irony of Thackeray,
The skill with a plot of Wilkie Collins.
Jane Austen has not the wit of Meredith,
The reforming energy of Charles Reade,
The imperial sense of Charles Kingsley,
The tender pathos of the author of *Cranford*.
And as for Mrs Gaskell who wrote *Cranford*
Well, she has not the aloofness of Jane Austen,
And Christina Rossetti had not
The manly optimism of Browning,
And Browning lacked the religious confidence
Of Christina Rossetti, or the serenity
Of Matthew Arnold. And who was Matthew Arnold?
Landor could not write about whist and old playbills
Like Charles Lamb.
(*Saint Charles, Thackeray murmured softly!*)

No one who has paid any attention at all
To the official-critical appraisements of English writers
Can gainsay the moral to be drawn
From these instances of depreciation
Or the truth of the projection itself.
Literary figures should, of course,
As is said of race-horses, be 'tried high',
But to attach a Derby winner to a stone cart,

And then condemn it as a horse
Because it does not make so much progress
As a Clydesdale or a Percheron
Is to try the animal
Altogether too high.
And not fairly.

English official criticism has erected
A stone-heap, a dead load of moral qualities.
A writer must have optimism, irony,
A healthy outlook,
A middle-class standard of morality,
As much religion as, say, St Paul had,
As much atheism as Shelley had . . .
And, finally, on top of an immense load
Of self-neutralizing moral and social qualities,
Above all, Circumspection,
So that, in the end, no English writer
According to these standards,
Can possess authenticity.
The formula is this: Thackeray is not Dickens,
So Thackeray does not represent English literature.
Dickens is not Thackeray, so *he*
Does not represent English literature.
In the end literature itself is given up
And you have the singular dictum
Of the doyen of English official literary criticism.
This gentleman writes . . . but always rather uncomfortably . . .
Of Dryden as divine, of Pope as divine,
Of Swift as so filthy
As to intimidate the self-respecting critic.
But when he comes to Pepys of course
His enthusiasm is unbounded.
He salutes the little pawky diarist
With an affection, an enthusiasm,
For his industry, his pawkiness,

His thumb-nail sketches
Then he asserts amazingly:
'This is scarcely literature'
And continues with panegyrics that leave no doubt
That the critic considers the Diary
To be something very much better.
The judgement is typically English.
The bewildered foreigner can only say:
'But if the Diary is all you assert of it,
It must be literature, or, if it is not literature,
It cannot be all you assert of it.'
And obviously . . .

I once met a Peruvian who had come
To London to study English literature.
He said: 'Oh! but your writers, they pant and they pant;
Producing and producing! And then, as the type,
The Archtype, you have . . .
Charles Lamb *On Buttered Toast!*'
I said: 'Ah! That is because
You are not an Englishman!'
So our business men pretend to take pride
In the quite false assertion that they have no time
For reading books . . . And so we remain
A blot on the world, and our populations
Are regarded as more and more suspect.
That is a misfortune because our writers,
Hampered as they are by political necessities,
By hypocritical and crystalized moralities,
And by commercial pressures, have yet,
As it were between the blasts of these storms,
Produced a great body of beautiful and humane work;
Enough to entitle us to occupy a place
In the comity of civilized nations.

Suppose a British Cabinet Minister or an American high politician
Were asked to stand up in a Walhalla of the nations
And claim for their twin civilizations
Their place in the sun,
On what achievements would he base their claim?
He would talk about the steam engine, the spinning jenny,
The steam-hammer, the electric telegraph, submarine cables,
The gramophone, the 'movies', wireless.
Being at this point probably coughed down
He would hazard, more dubiously, a new departure.
He would begin to talk of evolutions of freedoms
And moralities; of Houses of Representatives,
Of Congressmen, Commons, County Councils;
Of Colonial traditions, ballot-boxes, institutions,
Of perfecting the factory system,
Of modern industrial life which is nowhere so . . .
As for our favoured lands . . . the purity of . . .
In our great cit . . . initiation of legislation . . .
Against the White Slave Traf. . . . Anti-Alco. . . .
Non-Secret Dip. . . .

His voice being drowned, puzzled and irritated
He would cease, and in the eventually resulting silence
A kindly Scandinavian would be heard to prompt:
'Speak about Mr Shaw!'

'Oh! Ah, yes!' He would grasp at the proffered branch.
There's Shakespeare . . . and . . . Shakespeare . . . and Lord Byron
. . . But perhaps he's a little too . . . And . . .
Of course Shakespeare . . . and . . .
Did someone say Herbert Spencer? Yes, yes.
There are few branches of human activities in which
By the temperate employment of non-sectarian religion
In social problems our favoured nations. . . .

And so our cases go by default!

It is not in that way that the rest of the world
Frames its *apologia*. In the forefront
Of *Toutes les Gloires de la France* are set
Not merely the names of Napoleon, the Great Condé,
Le Roi Soleil, or merely Pasteur, Robespierre,
Danton or Lafayette; it is not merely by the names
Of Bismarck, Moltke, Marx, or Ehrlich
That Germany claims pity from Europe;
Nor does Italy ask patience solely
Because of Mazzini, Garibaldi, Savonarola;
Nor Russia only because of Peter the Great,
Schuvalof, Bakunin, Kerensky, or Lenin;
Nor yet is it because of the names
Of Ginaclis, Thetocopoulos, or Venizelos
That the name of Greece survives among the nations;
Nor will the names of Rosebery, Haldane, Balfour
The Earl of Elgin, Sir James Lithgow, the present Lochiel,
Lord Bilsland, Tom Johnson . . . quicken a spark of life
In the once-great-name of Scotland again,
Nor the Duke of Buccleuch, the Earl of Strathmore, the Earl of
    Airlie
Or any of the famous fatheads . . . any name at all
Known to a fraction of one per cent of the Scottish people,
Our blatant vulgarians of business men,
Our brainless bankers and lawyers
Our puerile Professors and dud Divines,
And all our other 'loyal Kikuyu'

(Call the roll of our M.P.'s to-day,
All our peers and public men
. . . And public women too . . . of every kind.
A single little-known name outweighs the lot,
Is of infinitely more consequence
To everything worth calling Scotland . . .
The name of Father Iain of Barra!

Or think of Cunningham-Graham whose magnificent presence
And flashing wit these hoodlums hated like Hell
Because it showed them what sub-men they are,
How horribly infra-human in comparison;
Cunninghame-Graham whose passing has left Scottish life
More mean and gray than ever before.

Yes, I still retain a little
Of the vehmic type of mind,
The 'raucle tongue', and *Hohngelachter*
That has characterized my folk so long.

And weigh my friend Ruaraidh Erskine of Marr
Against all the massed battalions of those
Who know nothing of Gaelic civilization and culture
And yet decry both
. . . Or against those others of whom as of the lady
Who wrote a book on the Lords of the Isles
It had to be said
'Tha cuid de'n sgriobhadh anns an leabhar so boidheach ri
leughadh, ach is mor am beud nach robh na's fearr colas aig a'
    bhan-ughdair air a' chuis.')

Indeed such names as these, of thinkers and of
Men of action in fields purely material
Are the names that separate Europe into nations . . .
They provide the separate glories of France, Italy,
The Alemannic peoples, Greece . . . but the others,
The glorious names of all the imaginative writers
From Homer to the Brothers Grimm,
From Flaubert back to Apuleius,
From Catullus to Turgenev,
All these form the glories of Europe,
Their works going together to make one whole,
And each work being one stone
In a gigantic and imperishable fabric.

It is possible that a change may come,
In the general revaluation that is taking place
All the commercial considerations, the moral greasinesses,
The Professors of Literature, *Vorschungen*, university curricula,
Honours examinations, all these phenomena commercial at base
Which stand in the way of the taste for
And honouring of literature
May be estimated at their true price.

To seek to abolish them is not much good.
For they are parts of the essential imbecilities
Of pompous men – of the highly refined imaginations
Of the More Select Classes.
They should be left isolated in little towns
But their existence should not be forgotten
Or they will come creeping in again.

Scots Unbound

Divertissement Philologique

Cwa: think o' nocht but the colours then
And catch me in the trebuck, lad.
English words are wide o' the mark
In a viese like this, b'Gad,
O' hasart bennels and falow breckan
– Juist ettle through yon far wuds
The divers degrees and shades to reckon
O' umbrate, thester, and mark, to the cluds
            At last they wallow in,
Or in the pyrnit fields that to ozmilt dwine
            Or in the waters that rin,
Sae lang submerged but on the skyline
            Kyth wips o' orpine afore they're din;
            Syne let's begin
If we're to dae richt by this auld leid
            And by Scotland's kittle hues
To distinguish nicely 'twixt sparked and brocked,
Blywest and chauve, brandit and brinked,
And a' the dwaffil terms we'll need
            To ken and featly use,
Sparrow-drift o' description, the ganandest gait,
Glaggmuha ἀκριβῶς, to dae as we ocht,
Bring oot a' the backward tints that are linked
Frae purpie to wan in this couthless scene
            – You see what I mean!
English is owre cauld-casten-to
For the thochts that Scotland should gar us brew.

            Warth skura windis mikila,
            Withondans haubida seina.
            Trudan ufaro waurme.

91

Krimi, carmine and crimson;
Κόκκος, cochineal, vermis, vermilion.
Bestail, grains, vins, fruictz
Haithi, timrian, thaurnus, blowans,
Fani, hugs. Hwaiwa us siggis?
  Silence, come oot o' him!
  Keep oot, che' vor ye!

Be a' that's jonet, sarrigold, orenze,
Rudede, moriane, katmogit,
Emeraud, endorrede, and electre,
Blae and mouskit, resplaid in oor verses yet,

Wi' blanket, blanchard, sorrit, reve,
Bassynt ga'en ghaist in the sun-fire,
And lattoun, lech as greenstane or trapp,
– Ilk Macklike, landrien, shire.

But colour in Scotland's owre thrawn and obscure
  For the een to ha'e the chief say?
Let's try smell then, and the sense o' taste
  Sae often bound up wi't tae.
Can you name as you turn your nose to a wind
  Or look in the opposite airt
This odour and that that's blended wi't
  And hoo each plays its separate pairt?

Some through the nosetirls alane and some
  Mair through the nerves o' the mou',
– Hoo a bricht licht's nim while a flann or youm
  Affects the throat like lamoo,
  Or the air like butter whiles has a gout,
Or a black soss hotterin' in the sun,
Ugg iper, gars you grue or gant?
Fegs, you're on dour and attrie grun'
(Dour, ordure, oh! durus amor!)

And you'll chowl wi' mony a smirkan here
As you catch this snoak or the ither;
      And the words you want,
Oorie and nesh eneuch, I fear,
'Ll tak' an unco gettin' thegither
As you get a youk frae some broc-faced place
Or the world gangs a' knedeuch in your face;
And, certes, it's only in Scots you'll find,
Tho' few can use them, words o' the kind.
Blaw ye south! man, for forsooth,
Here your tongue's awak in your mouth.
– 'I'll-thief, blaw the beggar south,
And never drink be near his drouth'
Mak' nae mistalk. Properlics similar to these
Ha'e diffcrent effects in Eire a'thegither
Whaur 'nae wits harden in the misty rushes,
Broon bogs, hills o' granite, magenta heather.'

Mony a natkin to kittle your mums;
And, withoot ony weasel-blawin',
A knaggin here and a yowther there
Has you hwindle-faced or gruntle-thrawn!
Mony a thocht the result o' a cens
A body's nose is owre deef to tell?
Mony a sairing, muff and foost
That words can gi'e nae magdum o'?
Haud on! We'll mak' them morigerate yet
And mair than sic nek-herring show,
Or naked neked, that's a' maist folk ken
– Wi' serpent-tongues in oor salers again.

You see or ken nocht withoot sensations o' touch
   Or the subtlest effects upon you o' shape.
Even aboot things you've never touched,
    Forms that a' nameable forms escape?
There's mair in the feel o' things than's kent by the hands,

Mair in their look than een can see,
　　That neist to naebody understands
Or due wecht to them can gi'e.
　　For want o' a' jedgry.
Hence a' oor kittle Scots words, hair splittin',
Nice shades o' meanin', aye closer fittin'
Ganand, in rayndoun, 'mair slink in the turn,'
And the way wi' a landscape we see oorsels in it,
　　　　　　Ken it in terms o' oor mombles faur mair
　　　　　　Than we're often, if ever, aware,
　　　　　　The vivisection o' the word made flesh
　　　　　　Is eneuch to mak' ony man nesh.
No' the Esk that rins like a ribbon there
But gi'es and tak's wi' the cluds in the air
And ootwith its stent boonds lies at the root
O' the plants and trees for miles roonaboot,
And gethers its tributaries, yet pulse-beats back
Up through them and a' that mak's it helps mak'
Sae I wad that Scotland's shape 'ud appear
As clear through a' its sub-shapes here
As whiles through my separate works I see
　　　　　　Their underlyin' unity;
Even as a workman automatically sees
A' that belangs to his craft in a scene,
A' done – to do – possibilities,
Be it forestry, drainage, or fermin', gi'en,
Or a man versed in history anither lacks
An atmosphere o' associations mak's,
A special climate transformin' it a',
Oor nature's unconscience goal, oor bias,
Advances this and recedes the ither,
And sae their influences upon us fa',
Feed us or fail us, and in a' ways try us,
And country and consciousness mell thegither.
　　　　　　Misk, and misgar, wi' nebawae life,
　　　　　　　And nig-ma-nies o' floo'ers,

94

It tak's nae ogertfow poet to sing
Sic a wowf and wurl-like land as oors;
– But nae 'Northman's thing made South-folk's
    place'
Is worth a curse in ony case!

Sae my mind hawk-steadies owre the moor
'Mang the glorifluikins and gloffs o' a lift
Owre big ne gnede. But what obiuse
Atour me gars the universe shift,
What gylooms range its glents and glooms,
Investigabill tows o' the rack o' cluds,
Upcastin' here and thorter there,
That in cat's hair streams or pack-merchans scuds
    I ken nae mair than a wag-string here.
    A feckless raipfu' as ever you saw,
A conjunct-feftment o' earth and air,
Tho' my oralog has nae moyne ava',
Nor houpitas for the stars or sun
Or the frape and frawarschip o' the grun'
                Wi' its gads o' ice and helms o' weet,
                Fires o' stanes and battles o' straw,
                Bands o' whins, and, tring by tring,
                A' its pry withoot jedgry there.
Noblay and nooslan in turn I tak
But baith determined ahint my back,
Couped frae a hule nae man can see
Whether earth-fast or howyn like me,
Tho', unlike maist, my muse gars't seem
That time itsel' has me hemilled roond,
Kennable and changin', no' borrell, space,
And that I hing in a livin' lift
Aye renewed and reshaped wi'in itsel;
And dedicate to the deemless scheme
O' the transformations o' a soul, hecht
The soul of extension, that has nae boond,

95

Sheer plenitude wi' its prevert face,
A quenchless flame that fills the haill place,
And lichts and warms me perthrough as I drift
          In nae perpetua clad
          Through schene and swaar
      But on fedren faw, like a watergaw,
          Wi' a' the colours there are
      – Or struggle syne, in a backthraw
Owre a world gane harth and haw.

Cwa; think o' nocht but the subtlest skills
Gubert in folk like you and me,
Kennin' hoo language, a tortoise competin'
Wi' licht's velocity, compares wi' sicht,
Tho' we canna imagine life withoot it,
Weird world-in-the-world, and seldom think richt
      O' the limitations no' lettin't gi'e
In libraries as muckle's in the turn o' an e'e,
Till whiles it seems there isna a taet
In a' creation it couldna state
But the neist instant we ken hoo sma'
A pairt o' life can be voiced ava',
– Nae words for the simplest experiences even,
Sae that, set doon in oor best freen's mind,
A terra incognita we'd find
          Yont a' believin'
Wi' here and there some feature we kent
But baffled whichever airt we went
Wi' unexpected groupin's, proportions, shapes,
Mismarrows through which a' sense escapes.
Kennin' my slughorn and a' my strynds
The language side o' sic gulfs lures me maist
Wi' words inouth, nane speaks or minds
Withoot muckle keach, afore me raised
In shapes that excite or dow me mair
          Than ocht in the world ootby there.

A' horns to the lift; cat's horns upmaist!
        But muckle that faceless lurks
In yon subdominal scene is no' to be faced?
        Your spirit the fell task shirks?

Cwa; think o' nocht but the colours then.
            It's the easiest way.
    Nigro-ruber, nigro-coeruleus,
    Dacklei, gule, blue day,
Sheep's lichtnin', dim-top brilliants, stopango gems,
– Nae mair o' your uchhas, imphms, and hems;
We'll tak' the country on oor backs,
    Green breese and crammasy cow,
    Richt through to black-be-lickit,
And whummle ony luppen rainbow I trow
    In the bowl o' oor occipitit;
And back again. Licht lifts the world's fax.
    The lucken-browed bront
    O' Scotland's on't.
Cwa; think o' nocht but a'thing then
And catch me in a trebuck, lad,
English words are wide o' the mark
    In a viese like this, b'Gad!

Jeannie MacQueen

O she was full of loving fuss
When I cut my hand and the blood gushed out
And cleverly she dressed the wound
And wrapt it in a clout.

O tenderly she tended me
Though deep in her eyes I could tell
The secret joy that men are whiles
Obliged to bleed as well.

I thanked her kindly and never let on,
Seeing she could not understand
That she wished me a wound far worse to staunch –
And not in the hand!

Two Memories

RELIGION? Huh! Whenever I hear the word
It brings two memories back to my mind.
Choose between them, and tell me which
You think the better model for mankind.

Fresh blood scares sleeping cows worse than anything on earth.
An unseen rider leans far out from his horse with a freshly-skinned
Weaner's hide in his hands, turning and twisting the hairy slimy thing
And throwing the blood abroad on the wind.

A brilliant flash of lightning crashes into the heavens.
It reveals the earth in a strange yellow-green light,
Alluring yet repelling, that distorts the immediate foreground
And makes the gray and remote distance odious to the sight.

And a great mass of wraithlike objects on the bed ground
Seems to upheave, to move, to rise, to fold and undulate
In a wavelike mobility that extends to an alarming distance.
The cows have ceased to rest; they are getting to their feet.

Another flash of lightning shows a fantastic and fearsome vision.
Like the branches of some enormous grotesque sprawling plant
A forest of long horns waves, and countless faces
Turn into the air, unspeakably weird and gaunt.

The stroke of white fire from the sky is reflected back
To the heavens from thousands of bulging eyeballs,
And into the heart of any man who sees
This diabolical mirroring of the lightning numbing fear falls.

Is such a stampede your ideal for the human race?
Haven't we milled in it long enough? My second memory

Is of a flight of wild swans. Glorious white birds in the blue October
   heights
Over the surly unrest of the ocean! Their passing is more than music
   to me
And from their wings descends, and in my heart triumphantly peals,
The old loveliness of Earth that both affirms and heals.

Vestigia Nulla Retrorsum

In Memoriam: Rainer Maria Rilke 1875–1926

Halophilous living by these far northern seas
How shall our sweetgales or Iceland poppies show
Their sympathy with your cleistogamic flowers,
  Or this barogouin of ours
Save as a tawny frogmouth cry
  Simultaneous with your nightingale?
Yet our abreption from the abderian accidie
Of most men brings us near you; we too go
Where no way save Alsirat can avail.

We too drank beer once in the common world
But not without acorus in it ever;
Knew women in maidenhead, maternity, and menopause,
  But know them better where none has
Entered since Time began or ever can
Save in our gynandromorphic moods. But soon
Our chalones parted us from that life of Man
Till crag-and-tail we stood with towering cliffs that sever
Us from Earth but elsewhere turn low green slopes and boon.

We set your image upon a naked stone
At our lectisternium here, with immarcescible flowers,
Since they are fashioned solely from the darkness and the light,
In such wise as is pleasing in the sight
Of our not-inexpert laevorotatory muse;
In such wise as – at other angles to the sun –
In paying homage you were wont to use;
And note its subtle changes through the moving hours
Yet save for the most obvious have scarce begun.

A naked stone that from the castle wall
Of Duino itself riven might be brought here to serve!

And yet no different from many another stone
Of this small island incredibly grey and lone.
Valéry did not know how you could bear to live
In that old stronghold of silence visible.
We do, who know the response our own bare stones can give,
Each turning in the sunlight to a naked nerve,
A brief boustrophedon of Heaven and Hell.
No more is interposed between God and us
But the last difference between human and divine,
And yet we have not chosen between Heaven and Hell,
Too alive to both. When but the last films of flesh fell,
When we were in the world and yet not in it,
And the spirit seemed to waver its eyas wings
Into the divine obscurity, it could not win it.
We would not, if we could, the difference resign
Between God and us – the God of our imaginings.

In shades of lastery and filemot and gridelin,
Stammel and perse, our chesil and turbary lie
Far from Scotland, that land of liripoops we left
    On these sterile stones, all else bereft,
To watch the lacertine gleams, the lightning hummers, still.
Nature with her excessive being no more could come
Over us here, we thought, as prophecy over Paul;
Lagophthalmic as God himself we yet descry
Overwhelming nimiety in this minimum!
What logodaedaly shall we practise then?
What loxodromics to get behind the light?
Glistening with exoskeletal stars we turn in vain
This way and that and but changing perigraphs gain,
Parablepsies, calentures, every cursèd paranthelion
Of this theandric force Pepper's ghosting God.
There is an accidie in all acceptance shown.
Is this God cheating too? Yet we will not. The fight
Continues under next to nothing's still more hopeless load.

We cannot read this qupu of the air,
This ogham on the stones, even as geologists fail
To tell from the striae which of two opposite ways
The ice went; and all upon which we can gaze
Is as obvious as the effects of the Flood and yet
Its waters did not penetrate very deep
Nor disturb Earth's strata much; nor will thought deeper get.
Even as rustics deplore an early spring – yet hail,
So we all hope of God repudiate – and keep.

But ah! there is an accidie in the fight as well.
The edge of the sword becomes serene in our hands.
This is no less an acceptance; and we know
A kindred peace in the heart of the conflict glow;
The cyclone's centre is a core of peace.
We too have fallen in the sink of swords,
Stricken suddenly with love of our enemies,
The stupid end no human ingenuity withstands
Alike to deeds and words and lack of deeds and words.

We would not if we could, but must we when we can?
Is this the sorry end of all our subtleties,
Unconscious compromise, natural yielding, brute collapse?
Our lost origin our acropetal striving saps.
Or human consciousness seems to us
Like thunder through successive banks of fog to go
Bubbling up between them furious
And muffled again; and among these mysteries
We poets sit ceraunic as a chalumeau.

Nor twissel-tongued can we penelopise;
Shut our eyes despite their madarosis of the sun.
Any island's too small for more than life and death.
And in the darkest night with bated breath
To grope our way over familiar stones made foreign

By any parapsis in a petty Ragnarok
Will not avail us. Such paraplegias we have borne
While over us Heaven's last lauwines seemed to run
– Only the scaphism of the stars anew to brook!

Why

Concerned as I am with the West Highlands and Hebrides
Instantly to my hand is the fact
That the two greatest social and religious reformers
Of modern India – Dayanandi and Gandhi –
Were both born in the small peninsula of Kathiawar.
Gandhi was born at Porbunder.
It is on the sea-coast, jutting out into the sea,
And has all the infinite variety and charm
Of the expanse of ocean around it.
Mists of extraordinary beauty
Constantly rise from the sea
And encompass the land,
The sea itself is usually a brilliant ultramarine
With liquid green where the shoals lie.
The little town where Gandhi was born
Rises almost out of the sea
And becomes a vision of glory at sunrise and sunset
When the slanting rays beat upon it,
Turning its turrets and pinnacles into gold.
Morvi, where Dayanandi was born, lies inland
Not far from the desolate waste
Of the Rajputana Desert which stretches to the North
Unbroken for hundreds of miles.
The land at Morvi is rocky
And the country is rugged,
The differences of their birthplaces are clearly seen
In the differences between Dayanandi and Gandhi.
We have Porbunders and Morvis enough
In Scotland: but they produce
No such outstanding characters
As Dayanandi and Gandhi,
Why?

My Songs are Kandym in the Waste Land

Above all, I curse and strive to combat
The leper pearl of Capitalist culture
Which only tarnishes what it cannot lend
Its own superb lustre.

Somewhere in its creative faculty is concealed
A flaw, a senseless and wanton quality
That has no human answer.
An infernal void.

Capitalist culture to the great masses of mankind
Is like the exploitative handling in America
Of forest, grazing, and tilled lands
Which exaggerates floods and reduces
The dry-season flow of the rivers to almost nothing.

A hundred million acres, which might have maintained
A million families, utterly destroyed by water erosion,
Nine million acres destroyed by wind,
Hundreds of millions of acres more
Yielding rapidly to wind and water erosion,
Forests slashed to the quick
And the ground burned over,
Grazing lands turned into desert,
The tragic upsetting of the hydrologic cycle
Which has turned into disastrous run-off
The water that should have been held in the soil
To support vegetation and percolate
To the lower levels and feed wells and springs,
Till now the levee builders try to raise
The Mississippi and set it up on stilts
Whence sooner or later it must stumble.

Problems of erosion control, regulation of river-flow,
Flood control, silt control, hydro-electric power.
I turn from this appalling spectacle
Of illimitable waste; and set myself, they say,
Gad im ghainimh (putting a withy round sand).
The sand will produce a vegetation itself
If it is not interfered with. It will be a slow growth.
Nevertheless the vegetation manages to get a start
In the course of thousands of years,
And my poetry will be like the kandym
That doesn't advance step by step
But goes forward on the run, jumps through the air,
The little nut jumps along like a ball.
The sand comes along after, but the sand is heavier
And cannot catch up with the little nut
And bury it. But when the seed takes root
And the little shrub starts, the shrub
Cannot jump along like the seed ball.

How is it going to save itself
From the encroaching waves of sand?
It is not so easy to bury the kandym.
It doesn't have branches like those
Of the apricot and peach tree – its branches
Are slender and there are no leaves on them.
When the sand comes on the kandym doesn't try to stop it
But lets it go right through its branches,
Gives it right-of-way.

But sometimes the sand waves are so big
They bury the kandym nevertheless.
Then a race begins – the dune grows and the plant grows.
The dune grows fast but the plant grows faster still
And by the time the sand dune has attained its final height
The plant is found to have outstripped it.
Its little green bristles are waving in the wind

On the crest of the sand dune.
It has not only grown in height but has branched out too.
The whole dune is perforated with its branches.
The wave passes on, leaving behind
A good half of its sand.
So the little kandym has stopped the advance of the sand,
Turned the dune into a little hillock
Covered with vegetation.

But is there not one last danger?
The wind may blow the sand away
And leave the roots bare?
But the kandym knows how to fight with the wind too.
Lying flat on the sand it sends out extra roots
And holds the sand down with them.
In this way it gathers up the soil
And makes a foothold for itself.
My songs are kandym in the Waste Land.

This
Treasure Cove Story
belongs to

PIRATE PUPS!

A CENTUM BOOK 978-1-912841-44-8
Published in Great Britain by Centum Books Ltd.
This edition published 2019.

1 3 5 7 9 10 8 6 4 2

Centum Books Ltd, 20 Devon Square, Newton Abbot,
Devon, TQ12 2HR, UK.

www.centumbooksltd.co.uk | books@centumbooksltd.co.uk
CENTUM BOOKS Limited Reg. No. 07641486.

A CIP catalogue record for this book is available
from the British Library.

Printed in China.

Centum

A Treasure Cove Story

PIRATE PUPS!

Based on the teleplay 'Pups and the Pirate Treasure'
by Ursula Ziegler Sullivan

Illustrated by Fabrizio Petrossi

One day, while exploring the cliffs above Adventure Bay, Cap'n Turbot slipped and fell down a dark hole. At the bottom, he discovered an old pirate hideout.

He was stuck in the creepy cavern, but he knew who could help him: the PAW Patrol!

Ryder called the PAW Patrol to the Lookout and told them about Cap'n Turbot.

'He's stuck in a cavern filled with pirate stuff, and he thinks it might be the hideout of the legendary Captain Blackfur!' Ryder said. 'No one knows what he looked like or what happened to his treasure.'

Ryder needed Chase and Rubble for the
rescue, but he told the rest of the pups
to be ready, just in case.

Rubble was excited. He really wanted
to be a pirate!

Ryder, Chase and Rubble raced to the cliffs and
found the hole.

'Chase,' Ryder said, 'I need your winch hook
to lower me into the cave.'

'Chase is on the case!' He pulled the hook over, and
Ryder locked it onto his safety belt.

Chase carefully lowered Ryder into the dark hole.

The pups joined Ryder and Cap'n Turbot down below. Using Chase's spotlight, they found cool pirate stuff – a telescope, a flag and a real pirate hat! Ryder put the hat on Rubble's head.

'*Arr!*' said Rubble. 'Shiver me timbers!'

Chase sniffed the air. 'I smell seawater,' he said.
He followed the scent and discovered a secret passage!
But it was blocked by rocks.

'That must be the way to the beach,' said Ryder.

'Stand back, landlubbers!' said Rubble as he cleared
the way with his digger.

Ryder and the pups followed the passage to a beach.
They found an old bottle with part of a map inside it.
'Is it a pirate treasure map?' Rubble asked.
'Could be,' said Ryder. 'We need all paws on deck
to solve this mystery.'

Ryder called the rest of the pups to the beach and told them that the map had been torn into three pieces.

'There's a clue to where we'll find the next piece,' he said. *'The part of the map that you seek hides in the big parrot's beak.'*

The pups thought about the clue. Suddenly, Rocky
said, 'Those boulders at the bottom of Jake's Mountain
kind of look like a parrot!'
'Let's check it out,' Chase barked.

The team hurried to the rocks that looked like
a giant parrot. Skye flew up and found a bottle
in its beak. Another piece of the map was inside!

Rocky taped the pieces together, and Ryder
read the next clue: 'From atop Parrot Rock,
look towards the sea. A clue hides in the hollow
of a very big tree.'

'If we can solve that clue,' Ryder said, 'we should find Blackfur's treasure!'

Chase thought for a moment. 'The biggest trees around are in Little Hooty's forest.'

'Good thinking!' Ryder exclaimed.

The forest was filled with lots of big trees, so
Chase asked Little Hooty if he had seen an old bottle
in any of the branches. He had!
Little Hooty fluttered up to a hole high in a tree.

Marshall drove his fire
truck to the base of the tree,
extended the ladder and
climbed up.
'Little Hooty was right!'
he said. He took down a bottle
that contained the last piece
of the map.

Rocky taped the pieces together. They now had the whole map! Ryder read the final clue: *'Walk twenty paces from the tree towards setting sun and rising sea.'*

Ryder turned to face the sun and the sea and he started walking.

From the edge of the cliff, Ryder and the pups saw something amazing through the fog.

It was an old pirate ship next to
a deserted island!
'Do you think it's Captain Blackfur's
ship?' Rubble asked.

The PAW Patrol worked together to pull the ship onto the beach.

News of the find spread through Adventure Bay. Mayor Goodway and her pet chicken, Chickaletta, came to see the exciting discovery.

On board, Ryder, Cap'n Turbot and the pups found
an old treasure chest. Inside were coins, jewels, a gold
bone and even a fancy dog bowl.

'Why would a pirate captain have a dog bowl?'
Marshall asked.

Then, digging through the treasure, Ryder found
an old picture of Captain Blackfur.

Captain Blackfur was a pirate pup!
'He looks just like me, except with a *black fur* beard!'
Rubble exclaimed.
The team let out a mighty *'Arr!'*
Three cheers for the pirate pups of the PAW Patrol!

Treasure Cove Stories

•Book list may be subject to change.